saving Cinderella

fairy tales & children
in the 21st century

RACHEL HOPE CROSSMAN

the apocryphile press
BERKELEY, CA
www.apocryphile.org

apocryphile press
BERKELEY, CA

Apocryphile Press
1700 Shattuck Ave #81
Berkeley, CA 94709
www.apocryphile.org

Table of Contents

*This book is for all of the teachers and parents
who don't believe in fairy tales.*

It is dedicated to:

*my husband Rob,
my four children,
my animal helpers.*

Because I could not have written it without them.

Section One

Why Cinderella?

Introduction

The title of this book, *Saving Cinderella: Fairy Tales and Children in the 21st Century*, invites questions: "Why Cinderella?" "Why now?" "What's the big deal about fairy tales?" The short answer to all of them is because reading fairy tales is fun, and children who enjoy reading do more of it. Since good readers go on to become good students, maybe the secret to making kids better readers is to let them spend more time reading fairy tales and less time preparing for standardized tests.

The Cinderella story is a compelling one, describing just which chores Cinderella was made to work at, just which words her stepsisters chose to insult her with, and just how clever the girl could be in completing the impossible tasks she was often assigned. Cinderella stories often include vivid depictions of the consequences for those who have done the girl wrong, providing vicarious satisfaction for any child who has ever felt unfairly treated. Such dramatic action makes the story ideal for use with unmotivated readers or struggling readers, whether children or adult, as well as second language learners.

One meaning of this book's title is that too many of our children are *becoming* Cinderella. Inner city, urban schools seem to be the poor stepchildren of our nation. Those who attend them are poorly equipped to compete with their better-off counterparts in more privileged districts. The gulf that exists between those who read proficiently and those who do not is widening. For too many children, the harsh reality of school budget cuts, coupled with family stress, is impeding academic progress. As a result, they may be locked in poverty. We as a nation are figuratively dressing our children in rags.

The second meaning of the title is that of literally *saving* Cinderella and the panoply of fairy tales from being lost from our cultural consciousness. As the world of education tilts farther toward standards-based teaching, fairy tales and the imagination are being written out of the grade school experience. But there are good reasons for reading these stories. The medium for incubating joy in reading is world literature, and the archetypal imagery of fairy tales feeds the soul. Children love to read them because the themes of family, of striving to achieve greatness, and of struggling heroically against obstacles resonate with them today as much as they did with children a thousand years ago. Today's kids need these memories from humanity's collective unconscious for their holistic wellbeing.

This book aims to promote the joy of reading while building literacy skills in children and others learning to read English. The five Cinderella stories featured here are intended as an introduction to the genre. This book is ideal for use by adults who may not have learned to read for pleasure themselves and may be unfamiliar with fairy tale structure. It is especially addressed to teachers, and offers a resource to parents, grandparents, and anyone who wants to read more fairy tales. It gives a clear, simple overview of the meaning behind some common symbols, and is a one-volume education on the how and why of reading Cinderella. Thirteen animals, including birds, cats, cows and lizards, are examined for their places in world mythology and the Cinderella story. Five objects and elements, including pumpkins, shoes and spinning wheels, are explained in historic terms and defined as archetypal images. It is my hope that through greater understanding of the history and deeper meaning of fairy tales, these stories will find a stronger place in twenty-first century education.

While researching this book I began a blog where I posted a different version of the worldwide Cinderella story every day during the year 2011. That blog, *365 Cinderellas* is categorized by animal, country, and object, and includes lesson plans for use with children ages six through twelve. It profiles stories from more than forty countries, including Korea, Norway, Mexico, and the Philippines. It may be accessed at http://rachel-hopecrossman.blogspot.com.

Chapter One
Why Reading Fairy Tales Makes Better Readers

The idea that reading three or four different Cinderella stories can raise literacy scores among targeted groups is backed by science. The National Reading Panel, which was created by the United States Congress in 1997 to examine research on literacy, studies literacy education in America. It analyzes data and funds the reading programs that produce the best results. In 2000, their meta-analysis showed five categories of skills needed. Known today as the Five Pillars, they form the basis for the way reading is taught to children in the United States today. These are the skills that are necessary for closing the so-called "achievement gap" between the lower and higher economic ends of our society.

The Five Pillars of Literacy

Phonemic awareness means training the ears to hear and the mouth to speak the smallest bits of sounds that are language. Babies who say *goo-goo gaa-gaa* are practicing this skill, exercising the brain areas that control listening and speaking.

Research shows that the ability to accurately isolate and reproduce individual sounds is the first pillar of literacy.

Phonics is the skill of matching sound and symbol. The ability to read and write the twenty-six letters of our alphabet and knowing all their different sounds is the foundation for all future reading and the second pillar of literacy.

Fluency is being able to read smoothly without stumbling and stopping. Good readers hear the language in their mind as clearly as their own voice when they speak aloud. Some people find this skill hard to learn, and now we know why. Studies show that reading fluently means doing three things at once. The first sub-skill is learning to control the speed, or *rate*, as you read. When it takes a long time to sound out each word, the meaning of the sentence, never mind the story, gets lost. Faster is better.

The second sub-skill is *prosody*, which means feeling the beat of the language. Rhyming words and repeating patterns in poetry and prose help emerging readers get a feel for how the words should sound when spoken aloud.

People who can recognize words at a glance are at a strong advantage in reading. *Automaticity* is the third sub-skill of fluency, and it means reading whole words, not letters. The less attention a child spends sounding things out the more he or she can spend enjoying the story.

Vocabulary is the fourth pillar of literacy. Words a child knows by heart are like dollars in a bank account. The more they have, the richer they will be. But truly learning new words doesn't mean just memorizing them from lists. Matching a new word with some old knowledge is the way to make it stick, which is why language needs to be learned through activity. A child who notices that the sky is blue and the grass is green, and then draws a picture of it makes a stronger memory. If he writes a sentence about the sky and the grass, the words *blue* and *green* are then tied to his drawing, and also to his memory of the blue sky and the green grass. It will be easy for this child to expand his vocabulary of color, for example, by learning that sometimes the sky is also gray or white or black.

Vocabulary must be built not only by naming what we see and hear and feel, but through reading books. In fact, research has shown that the bigger a child's vocabulary, the better a reader he will be. This makes sense because the more words he knows, the better he can follow the story. Often kids who don't like to read don't know enough words to keep up with the action. It turns out that a big part of the infamous "achievement gap" is actually a vocabulary gap. Reading fairy tales in general, and the worldwide Cinderella story in particular, is a great way to build vocabulary and fluency.

Reading for Understanding

Learning to understand a story's arc—identifying the beginning, middle, and end of it—is a skill good readers have. Reading the same story again and again is a useful tool for acquiring this understanding because it ties something that is known with new information.

Chapter Two
Fairy Tales, Some History

Before electronic entertainment—before human-kind knew how to light up the night as brightly as day—sharing stories by the fireside was what people did for fun. Often the elders of a community were the repository of oral histories, as well as family secrets and tall tales. Younger people and children listened to the stories of times gone by, as told by Grandma or Great-Uncle Somebody-or-Other. Certain stories are told all over the world. On every continent, in every time period, folk tales and fairy tales exist.

According to Marie Louise von Franz, an associate of Dr. Carl Jung, fairy tales are a genre defined separately from myths and legends. The latter have grown up from "local sagas" which are based upon a kernel of truth. That truth may be several generations from the primary source, but it still rings with familiarity for people native to a particular area. Von Franz cited as an example of this phenomenon a castle located in the countryside, around which a story is told of the people who once lived there, and the tragedy that befell them. The characters involved were human beings, confronted with real life situations.

The characters in fairy tales are stereotypical and one-dimensional. There is no shivering and shaking in the dark, no agonizing over right or wrong. The princess escapes or the hero slays the monster without a second thought. It is this deceptive simplicity that makes them so powerful. Von Franz said:

> Fairy tales are the purest and simplest expression of collective unconscious psychic processes. Therefore, their value for the scientific investigation of the unconscious exceeds that of all other material. They represent archetypes in their simplest, barest, and most concise form. (1996)

Dr. Carl Gustav Jung was the founder of depth psychology, which strives to understand the contributions that the unconscious makes to our personality and daily functioning. He believed that the human psyche, though limitless in what it can produce, seems to come with some library images from humanity's shared narrative. By studying world literature and religions, he confirmed that humankind has, since time immemorial, conceptualized the internal life of the mind in ways recognizable to modern culture. Jung said:

> Man's unconscious archetypal images are as instinctive as the ability of geese to migrate in formation; as ants forming well-organized soci-

eties; as bees' tail wagging dance that communicates to the hive the exact location of a food source. (1979)

Jung brought to humankind the world of dreams, and the concept of the unconscious as a reservoir of creative thought.

Anthony Stevens, a Jungian analyst and psychiatrist from the University of Oxford, England, has continued the analysis of archetypal symbolism. In his 1998 book, *Ariadne's Clue: A Guide to the Symbols of Humankind*, he said:

> Symbols are living entities with a life-cycle of their own; they are born, flourish for awhile, then dwindle and die. New symbols come into existence all the time, but not in an arbitrary or unrelated way. They bear a family resemblance to each other and to their ancestors, in the sense that they are imaginal forms.

In other words, symbols have meaning only because we human beings give them meaning through the use of our unconscious imagination. The word that describes these universally recognizable characters and images is *archetype*. Human archetypes include *anima* and *animus*, the male and female elements of every human psyche, and they exist in four stages.

The primitive or child persona can include ogres, trolls, or kind-but-foolish youngest sons. The youth or maiden may be royal or not, attractive or ugly. Mother and Father are the caretakers, and do not always appear as a couple. Wise elders include governesses, hen-wives, helpful cooks and servants. They offer advice and give assistance, and may be called witches, healers, or medicine men. Each of these characters can be positive or negative; a child's innocence turns to brutishness and an elder's wisdom becomes poisonous spite.

The helpful birds, mice, lizards, and cows that solve impossible problems and lend improbable tools to damsels in distress are also of a known order, the *animal archetype*. Animals in fairy tales often are humans under spells. Creatures such as griffins, which are half lion and half eagle, or mermaids, which are half woman and half fish, show that the line between people and animals is often unclear. Jung wrote:

> The self is often symbolized as an animal, representing our instinctive nature and its connectedness with one's surroundings. That is why there are so many helpful animals in myths and fairy tales. (1979)

There are archetypal landscapes and objects as well. The foreboding castle, the endless waves of the sea, an impenetrable forest or a winding staircase all evoke emotional responses. Everyday household items, especially those which we use or wear often, acquire power. Anyone who has visited a museum to see the uniform worn by Napoleon Bonaparte, or King Tutankhamun's sandals, knows that. Objects become, in some mysterious way, extensions of the personalities of the people who use them, and carry their power. This is why in fairy tales, precious objects are given and received and clothing is often exchanged. The symbolism of rings with power and cloaks that conceal secrets can be explored and defined in much the same way that the details of human anatomy can be mapped.

Chapter Three
The World Wide Cinderella Story

Tales of girls with miserable lives but high hopes of better days are one of the oldest and most prevalent on earth. Cinderella is the archetypal maiden who, when confronted by those who wish her harm, keeps her cool and manages to achieve success. One of the first versions was recorded around the time of the birth of Jesus by a Greek scholar named Strabos. It is the story of a woman named Rhodopis, who was born a slave and buried as a queen. Her change in fortune was due to the chance theft of one of her shoes by a large bird. The shoe was carried, apparently, to the city of Memphis, before the bird tired of its weight, and let it go. The sandal landed right in the lap of the Pharoah, who was so intrigued by the event that he sought the woman who had the shoe's mate, found her, and then married her.

In China, the girl is called Yeh-Shen, an orphan who lived so long ago that the dynasties had not yet been founded. She is starved and abused by her stepmother, but manages to find friendship with a little fish. Spying on the girl one day, her stepmother discovers the fish, kills it, and eats it. When Yeh-Shen makes this heartbreaking discovery, a mysterious Kind Uncle appears, and tells her that the fish bones contain magic. She retrieves what's left of her friend, and learns that they will grant her wishes. Because her main problem is simple survival, Yeh-Shen asks only for rice, and so is fed each day. When she learns that the Cave Chief is to hold a festival, she wishes for fine clothing so that she can attend. The outfit produced by the fish bones is a cloak of feathers, and includes tiny, golden shoes. Yeh-Shen attends the party, loses a slipper, and is tracked down by the King, who marries her.

The use of magic bones, or the relics of the friendly animal helper, as the means of granting wishes is an ancient story element. It is found in parts of Europe and Africa as well as in Cinderella stories from Korea, Vietnam, India and the Philippines. Animal bones and horns used include those of cows, goats, and chickens.

All over Europe, folk tales were told about a widowed father with a young daughter. The gentleman remarries, to the misfortunate of his first child. Known collectively as Cinderella Stories, many of these were gathered together in Marian Roalfe Cox's 1892 collection, done on behalf of the English Folklore Society. Her book, *Cinderella: Three Hundred Forty-Five Variants of Cinderella, Catskin, and Cap O' Rushes* focused mainly on stories from Europe, but included several stories from Asia, Africa, and the Americas. That organization is still flourishing in the twenty-first century and the book is still available.

Cox defined the variant she called *Catskin* as stemming from pre-historic nature stories. They involve contrasts between night and day, and the seasons and celestial elements often play important parts. The girl is abused by being forced to flee from an "unlawful marriage," either to her father or a passing stranger.

In this story type, a man, sometimes a king, has a wife who is at death's door, and also a pretty little girl. Before the mother dies, she gives her daughter some trinkets, usually a ring, a thimble and a golden spindle. She begs her husband to promise that if he marries again, the new wife will conform to a specific condition, usually that she can wear a ring of the first wife's, or has a birthmark exactly like hers. The man agrees and his wife dies. When he tries to remarry, the only woman he can find who fulfills the conditions of the oath is his own daughter. When he announces his intentions, she is repelled, and refuses.

Typically she then seeks advice from an older woman, either her grandmother or a servant, who counsels her to consent to the marriage but delay it, if possible, by asking for three very special dresses. The first is often described as being silver, or like the moon, the second gold, or like the sun, and third of diamonds, like the stars. When the girl's father has produced each of these dresses, and it seems that there is no hope left, the adviser has one more idea. The girl must ask for a truly unusual cloak, made from many small or hard to find items.

Often she demands that it be made from animal fur, specifically from black or calico cats. Other times it is a cloak of crows' bills or fish scales. When the garment is produced, the girl realizes that the only way to escape from her father is to run away. Dressed in her strange cloak, with her special dresses safely hidden, she takes service at a neighboring castle under the name of Catskin. Often she becomes a kitchen maid, but sometimes she works as a goose girl or swine herd. Variations with cloaks of mice, rabbits, donkeys, or birds' feathers come from Scandinavia, Ireland, Italy, and Russia. In most stories, the girl attends three balls dressed in her secret finery, and hides the trinkets from her mother in food she cooks for the prince. It is by this means that she is recognized as well born herself, and is able to marry the prince.

One of the earliest Italian versions of Cinderella was published in 1634 by Giambattista Basile. The printing press that revolutionized the world in 1454 facilitated the spread of popular literature, but it took some time before anything other than bibles were being printed on Gutenberg's contraption.

By the 1500's, medieval fiction, including the work of Geoffrey Chaucer and Dante Alighieri, had circulated enough to inspire other story collections, now easy to mass-produce. Tales that had existed only in oral versions were being gathered into books, and Basile, a writer and entrepreneur, seized the opportunity to publish *Lo cunto de li cunti overo la trattenemiento de peccarille (The Tale of Tales, or Entertainment for Little Ones)*. The second part of the title reveals that children at that time were seen as short, inexperienced adults, rather than as tender minds to nurture.

Presented as a story cycle told over the course of five days, it is a bawdy, rowdy, deliberately shocking collection of narratives that became a bestseller. Told in Neapolitan dialect, it is laced with extravagant dialogue, including paragraph-long insults exchanged and curses pronounced. The story begins with an argument between a young man and an old woman. He berates her and she responds by flashing her bottom at him. Lurid descriptions of bodily functions, bloody retribution, and sexual innuendo bring Basile's characters to life in brilliant color. *Il pentamerone,* as the book became known, lists, for the Sixth Diversion of the First Day, an elaborate story called *The Cat Cinderella*. The heroine, Zezolla, first murders her tutor, then is abused by her governess, and finally, with the help of a date tree, marries the prince. Immediately preceding this tale is one called *The Flea*; that following it is *Goat-Face*. Translated into English by Sir Richard Burton in 1893 and reissued in 1943, it can still be easily obtained. Reading it to children, however, is not necessarily recommended.

By the late 1600's, French society had developed a taste for wonder tales, those old stories about magic, talking animals, and enchanting spells. These *contes de fées*, or fairy tales became the fashion in literary salons—and the more extravagant, the better. The French intelligentsia encouraged authors to meet weekly and read aloud for one another's amusement. One of the most skilled at the highly stylized retelling of old wives tales was a Parisian named Charles Perrault. He was the youngest of five brothers and the son of a member of parliament. His niece, Mademoiselle Lhéritier, was a regular participant in these salons, as were many other young women. Charles finished university studies at the age of fifteen and was practicing law at eighteen. But very soon his romantic mind rebelled against this stuffy career. He quit law to work as a secretary for his brother, and wrote poetry in his spare time. By 1660, at the age of 32, he had published several acclaimed books of verse. He gained further celebrity by composing sonnets in honor of King Louis XIV.

He found enough success as a writer of fairy tales to quit working for his brother and began a public debate called *The Quarrel of the Ancients and the Moderns*. He argued the case for enlightened modernism, believing that the pagan roots of the early French people could be successfully blended with progressive society. After ten years of literary arguments and printed skirmishes, King Louis XIV decided in favor of Perrault's opponents. These were the literary critics Boileau and Racine, whose doctrine of strict preservation of the classics with no room for creativity was to the royal liking.

Perrault carried on stylizing and embellishing French folk tales, and in 1697 published *Histoire ou contes du temps passé*. He took this opportunity to include morals at the end of each story, determined to get his views across, no matter that in the king's eyes he had lost the debate. So as not to make waves, however, he published this volume under the name of his son, Pierre Perrault.

The collection of eight tales included *Little Red Riding Hood, Bluebeard*, and *Cendrillon, ou le pantouffle de verre*, known in English as *Cinderella, or the Little Glass Slipper*. Perrault describes her as the daughter of a rich, recently widowed merchant, who is maltreated by his second wife and her daughters. She is pushed from her own room to make way for her stepsisters, who mock her heartlessly. He wrote that Cinderella "had no place to sit but among the cinders, which made her be commonly called in the house Cinderbreech; but the youngest who was not so rude and uncivil as the eldest, called her Cinderilla."

The girl is aided by "her godmother, who was really a fairy" and who prepares the ragamuffin to go to the palace. Using a pumpkin, rats, mice, and lizards, the godmother produces a carriage, a team of horses, footmen, and a coachman. Cinderilla thanks the old woman but asks, "Must I go thither as I am, with these ugly and nasty clothes?"

Only then are her rags and wooden shoes transformed "into cloth of gold and silver all beset with jewels: after this she gave her a pair of Glass Slippers, the finest in the world."

The story ends with Cinderilla, who is not only

lovely but very forgiving, inviting her stepsisters to move to the palace and marry noblemen.

One of two morals at the end of the tale is:

Without doubt it is a great advantage to have intelligence, courage, good breeding, and common sense. These, and similar talents come only from heaven, and it is good to have them. However, even these may fail to bring you success, without the blessing of a godfather or a godmother.

Perrault's story is notable not only for his moralistic ending. His is the first reference to Cinderella's slippers being made of glass. Some folklorists have questioned whether the word *verre*, meaning glass, could have been mistranslated or misspelled. The French word *vair*, or *striped*, sounds just like the word for glass, and so perhaps the two were confused at some point in history. Others feel that Perrault knew exactly what kind of shoes his ragged girl wore.

He was also the first to include the transformation of mice, rats, lizards and a pumpkin. Mice and rats would have been a constant presence, so their inclusion as helper animals is a logical one. Lizards and pumpkins are more unusual choices, but were probably based in Perrault's knowledge of religion and mythology.

A wealthy and well-educated writer who lived from 1628 to 1703, Charles Perrault experienced turbulent times. The Great Plague of 1664 devastated much of Europe by killing more than seventy five thousand people and causing many more to flee. Just two years later, London was nearly wiped out by fire, and eighty four of its churches, including St. Paul's Cathedral, burned. Hundreds of thousands of people were left homeless, and the population shifted and mixed all over the continent.

As an intellectual on the lookout for interesting stories, Perrault was probably inspired to use magic pumpkins and enchanted lizards from several sources. Sailors and explorers brought home news as well as gold. After traveling across the Mediterranean Sea, and eventually to the Caribbean, they would almost certainly have brought stories back with them, perhaps some that seemed fantastic.

It is known that Christopher Columbus, who made his famous trip in 1492, carried gourd seeds home. Sir Francis Drake, who sailed around the world in 1580, probably did too. It seems likely that legends about these strange plants and their huge seeds would have made the journey as well. The West Indies and Africa are filled with tales of magic calabashes, and stories about large fruits that reveal treasures when cut open are found in Corsica, Portugal, Greece, and Asia.

The European custom of carving large vegetables into hollowed-out lanterns for All Hallows' Eve is another connection between pumpkins and witchcraft. As for lizards, they are first cousins to dragons, creatures with a venerable history in both Western and Eastern lore. Whatever the origin of the pumpkin, mice, rats and lizards, they are now inseparable elements of the Cinderella story.

The other famous European variant of the Cinderella story is that collected by brothers Jacob and Wilhelm Grimm and published 1812. Titled *Aschenputtel*, or *Aschenbrodel*, it is a much more brutal tale than Perrault's pretty fluff. The Grimms collected their stories over the course of two decades, while working as university professors and royal librarians. Both published major academic works on German law and the structure of classical German linguistics in addition to their best selling folk tale collections. Their goal was to preserve the folk culture they saw eroding and to promote civic pride in the newly unified kingdoms of the Holy Roman Empire, which became Germany in 1806.

It was not until later versions of the two hundred seventy-nine stories they collected that they began to shape them specifically for children.

When Aschenputtel's mother dies and her father remarries, she is picked on by her new stepsisters and made to become their servant. Turtledoves and pigeons take the place of a fairy godmother, assisting Cinderella in picking lentils out of the ashes when her stepmother flings them there out of spite.

Her father brings her a sprig of hazel, which the girl plants and waters with her tears. It grows into a large tree, and white doves nest in it, throwing down fine clothes and little gold shoes for Cinderella when she wants to go to the ball. Later, her father assists the prince in hunting for the mysterious girl in the golden slippers by chopping down first a pear tree he has seen her climb into, and then the dovecote, or bird house. Finally, the prince lays a tar-trap on the palace steps, and so obtains one of the shoes. When the search party looking for the girl who can wear it gets to Aschenputtel's house, her sisters try it on first. This stepmother shows her naked greed for power as she assists her oldest daughter:

> The shoe was too small and she couldn't get her big toe in. So her mother handed her a knife and said: "Cut your toe off. Once you're queen you won't have to walk anymore." The girl cut her toe off and forced her foot into the shoe, gritted her teeth against the pain and went out to the king's son.

The prince falls for it, and is on the verge of marrying the sister, when the doves begin to sing, "Rocoo, rocoo, there's blood within the shoe! The foot's too long, the foot's too wide, that is not the proper bride!" Finally, Aschenputtel gets her chance and slips the shoe on. She and the prince are married and the stepsisters have their eyes pecked out by the turtledoves on the way home from the wedding ceremony. "Thus they were punished with blindness for the rest of their lives due to their wickedness and malice" (Opie I and Opie 2, 1974).

American Cinderella stories include tales such as *The Poor Turkey Girl*, from New Mexico, and *Soot Face Girl*. Both were collected orally by folklorists in the United States and Canada and later published. African Cinderella stories came to the states along with the people taken in slavery raids.

Retellings of these include *The Talking Eggs* and *Sukey and the Mermaid*, picture books by Robert San Souci. *Chinye: A West African Folk Tale*, was retold and published as a lushly illustrated children's book by Obi Onyefulu in 1994.

Two versions of the Cinderella story brought to the United States by immigrants from England and Scotland in the 17th century are *Ashpet* and *Catskins*. Folklorist Richard Chase collected them during visits to the Appalachian Mountain regions of North Carolina and Virginia and published them in 1948 as *Grandfather Tales: American-English Folk Tales*. Kings and Queens and Princes appear in them, showing the story's roots, though other characters just treat them like ordinary "rich folks."

The story of *Ashpet* shows the American soft spot for the underdog by showing sympathy for a "hired girl" kept by "rich folks." When the family's fire goes out, she is sent out to borrow coals from a witch-woman in the woods, who asks Ashpet to help her by combing her hair. Ashpet does so, and the witch magically does the girl's chores. There is a King's son who comes riding through the neighborhood one day, and a shoe-fitting test to pick his wife. Though Ashpet gets hidden under a washtub, she escapes and marries the prince. But the daughters of her former employer are so enraged by her success that they try to kill her. They invite her on a picnic, then desert her at a swimming hole where "Old Hairy Man" lives. He captures Ashpet and keeps her in a cave for awhile, until she outsmarts him.

The story of *Catskins* that Chase collected also casts the heroine as a hired servant, avoiding the notion of incest found in the European versions. Another change is the addition of an *s* to the name. In this variant, Catskins is too poor to fix her torn clothes so she patches them with the skins of cats, backwoods style. The man who wants to marry her is not her father, but her boss. Catskins puts on the wedding dress of his dead wife and wanders out in the garden. When he asks her to marry him she stalls him by asking for three special dresses. Her boss gets each dress quickly, but then she asks for his magical "flying box" too. Of course she flies away in it as soon as she gets it. She finds a job at the kitchen of a rich man and encounters his son three times. At the last dance at the party, he gives her a ring, but she runs away. Finally he is so lovesick for her that the doctor calls for all the girls of the area to bake cakes and bring them. Catskins bakes one and hides the ring inside.

Chapter Four
Five Cinderella Stories

Following are five versions of the Cinderella story, each of which represents a major variant. Although they may seem simplistic, they should not be seen as dumbed down versions, but rather as aids to reading the originals in their archaic language. That language is rich and wonderful and children will benefit by reading full-length, literary fairy tales themselves, or by having them read aloud. However, confusing vocabulary may detract from the reader's understanding. The purpose of these five stories is to awaken an interest in the Cinderella genre in particular, and fairy tales in general, and provoke in the reader a search for more.

For further notes on the original sources from which these five stories are drawn, please see *Notes On the Stories*. Included here are:

• *Cinderella*, a very simplified easy-reader based on the famous glass slipper version written by Charles Perrault in French in 1697.

- A simplified Perrault's *Cinderilla, or the Little Glass Slipper (Cendrillon, ou le pantouffle de verre).*

- *Aschenputtel,* the bloody German folktale collected by Joseph and Wilhelm Grimm and published in 1812.

- *Catskins,* an American Cinderella story, imported directly by English and Irish settlers in the Appalachian Mountains in the eighteenth century. It has a long oral history and was collected by folklorist Richard Chase in 1948.

- *Chinye,* an African folktale based on the 1994 picture book *Chinye: A West African Folk Tale* by Obi Onyefulu, as well as other African fairy tales.

Easy Reader Cinderella

Once upon a time there lived a girl whose name was Ella. Her mother had died when she was very small, and her father had married again. This lady had two girls of her own, and they joined Ella's family, becoming Ella's stepmother and stepsisters. But they were mean to her! They made her do all of the work. Every night they said that it was her turn to do the dishes, and every morning they made her mop the floor. Since they liked her bedroom best of all, they took it for themselves and made her sleep in the attic. They even took all of her clothes, so that soon, all she had to wear was rags. When those rags got dirty they would not let her wash them. Instead, they teased her and called her Cinderella. But she was still very pretty, and that made her sisters even more jealous.

One day, the family heard that the prince and his brother were going to have a fancy party, and that all the girls were invited. But Cinderella's stepmother and stepsisters said that she could not go. Then they put on their fanciest dresses and left her behind. Luckily for Cinderella, she had a fairy god-mother who appeared in the kitchen! She could do magic! The fairy godmother said that Cinderella could go to the party, as long as she was home by midnight. The fairy did magic then and turned a pumpkin into a wagon, some mice into horses, and a rat into a man to drive the wagon. Best of all, the fairy godmother turned Cinderella's old dress into a golden gown and her shoes into glass slippers.

Cinderella had lots of fun dancing with the prince, and he had fun dancing with her. He want-ed her to stay for the whole party, but she knew that she had to be home by midnight. When she heard the bells of the clock ring twelve times, she ran away. One of her sparkly glass slippers got lost, but the prince found it. He told his mother, who was the queen, that he wanted to marry the girl that the shoe fitted, but he could not find her. So the Queen told him that he should ask all of the girls who lived in town to try the shoe on. He did, but it did not fit any of them. Then his father, the King, said that the prince should ask all the girls who lived out in the country to try it on.

So the prince asked his servant to take the shoe around and have all of the girls out in the country see if it fitted. When he got to Cinderella's house, her stepsisters tried to put on the shoe, but it did not fit them.

Then Cinderella said, "May I have turn now?"

Her stepmother and stepsisters told her "No!" but the prince's servant let her try the shoe on any-way.

It fit! Then Cinderella took the other glass slipper out of her pocket, and put that on too. The fairy godmother used her magic to make the golden gown appear again, and Cinderella went to the palace and married the prince. They lived happily ever after.

Cinderilla or
The Little Glass Slipper

Once upon a time, in France, there was a gentleman who married for his second wife a mean woman, with a face as ugly as her heart. She had been married before, but her husband had died. She was left with two daughters, who were exactly like her in every way. The gentleman had a young daughter as well. She was a kind, loving girl, just like her mother had been.

Soon after moving in, her stepmother put this young girl to work with the hardest chores. The new stepsisters treated her like a servant girl. Each day, she washed the dishes and mopped the floors, dusted the furniture, and did the laundry. At night she slept in a tiny room at the top of the house. This garret with a straw bed was all she had. But her sisters had fancy bedrooms, with inlaid floors, and big beds with covers of newest fashion. Each of their rooms had a full-length mirror, while the youngest girl could not even peek at her own face. She had no looking glass, nor soft slippers, nor pretty gowns. But she was still prettier than her sisters.

She did her best to be patient with her stepsisters, and did not dare to tell her father how meanly they treated her. He would only have rattled her off with a scolding. The poor girl was no longer allowed to eat her meals at the family table. She had no other chair, so she sat among the cinders in front of the fireplace, and her dress became dirty and gray. Her oldest stepsister began to call her Cinderbreech, but the younger sister was not quite so rude. She called her Cinderilla instead. Even though Cinderilla's clothes were old and torn, she was still a hundred times prettier than her sisters. They got new clothes every week and never tired of showing them off.

It happened that the King decided to give a ball. He invited all of the richest men in town, and all of the prettiest maidens as well. Now Cinderilla had to work even harder. Besides the daily laundry and cleaning, her stepsisters wanted her to sew extra petticoats for them. Then she had to starch and iron them, so that her sister's ball gowns would stand stiffly out around their small waists. They ate almost nothing for two days before the party because they were so excited, and wanted to be slender. They talked endlessly of their clothes.

"I'll wear my red velvet suit, with French trimming," said the oldest sister.

"And I," said the younger, "will put on my gold flowered jacket, and my diamond belt, which is my favorite!"

Then they sent for the best hairdresser they could get. She washed and combed their hair, braided it, and twirled it high onto their heads. She made elaborate towers out of their braids and fastened them in place with double pins.

At last, it was the day of the ball, and Madame De la Poche came, with her brushes and creams and makeup for their faces. All afternoon the stepsisters had ordered poor Cinderilla to do so many tasks that her head spun. Now, finally, they were gone. She sat down among the cinders and started crying.

That's when she heard a voice! It was her godmother, asking what was the matter.

"Oh! I wish I could, I wish I could..." she tried to speak her wish aloud, but tears kept interrupting her.

Her godmother, who was a fairy, said, "You'd like to go to the ball, wouldn't you?"

"Oh, yes!" said Cinderilla with a great sob.

So the fairy sent her into the garden and told her to pick a *pompion,* which was a kind of pumpkin. Cinderilla went out and got the best one that she could find. She brought it to her godmother, although she did not understand what it was for. But the old woman scooped out all the inside of it and when she had hollowed out the rind, she tapped it with her wand. The pumpkin immediately was turned into a coach, covered all over with gold.

Then her godmother found six mice in the mousetrap, touched them with her wand, and turned them into a very fine set of horses. They were dappled gray, the same color as the mice but much more beautiful. But who would drive the coach? The fairy godmother found a rat and gave it a tap from the wand, and it turned into a fat jolly man that had the biggest beard and mustache Cinderilla had ever seen.

Now they needed servants for the carriage. Six lizards who were hiding near the water jugs were transformed into six footmen, and they jumped up behind the horses. They were handsome young men, and their uniforms had buttons and gold trim.

But Cinderella was still crying, so the fairy said, "You have a fancy coach and horses, and I have even given you servants to take you to the ball. Why are you still unhappy?"

And Cinderilla answered, "Must I go thither as I am, with these ugly and nasty clothes?"

So her godmother touched the girl's old dress with her wand, and instantly it turned into a dress made of gold and silver cloth, all covered with jewels. Then she gave her a pair of glass slippers, the only ones in the world. She warned her goddaughter to leave before the clock struck twelve, because at that time the magic would wear off. Her coach would become a pumpkin again, her horses turn into mice, and her servants would once more be lizards. As for her clothes and shoes, they would become ragged and dirty again.

The coach whisked her away, and when Cinderilla walked into the palace a hush fell because she was so lovely. The prince thought she was a princess from another country, and the King himself, as old as he was, could not help staring at her. He told the Queen quietly that it was a long time since he had seen such a beautiful girl. The prince danced with her and then gave her the best place to sit.

But Cinderilla looked over and saw her sisters at

a different table, and went to see them. The prince had shared some delicious oranges and lemons with her, and she gave some of these to her stepsisters. They thanked her nicely, since they did not know who she was.

Suddenly, Cinderilla heard the clock chime eleven and three quarters. She curtsied to the prince and ran away as fast as she could. Back at home among the cinders, she changed clothes, thanked her god-mother, and begged to go again the next night. The fairy said that she could, and disappeared. Soon her sisters came home, and her older sister Charlotte teased her about the fun she had missed. Cinderilla did not care. But, to keep from making her sisters suspicious, she asked to borrow a dress and begged to go to the ball the following night. When they told her that no one would lend a gown to a Cinderbreech who would only get it dirty, she tried to look sad.

The next day, all three sisters were at the ball. Cinderilla's fairy godmother gave her a dress even more luxurious than the first one. The King's son stayed close beside her, and the two of them had so much fun talking and dancing that Cinderilla forgot to watch the time. When the clock struck twelve she was very surprised, so she cried out and ran away. As nimbly as a deer, she scampered out of the palace. The Prince followed her, but could not catch her. The only thing he found was one of her little glass slippers. He picked it up very careful-ly and looked around, but Cinderilla had vanished.

At home again her stepsisters gossiped about the

party. They said they had heard that the Prince was very much in love with the mysterious princess, and that the princess wore glass slippers, and had left one behind. And this was true, for just a few days later the King's son announced that he would marry the maiden whose foot the glass slipper fit. He ordered first that all the princesses should try it on, and then the duchesses, and then all the fine ladies of court. But no one could get the shoe on. At last, it was brought to the all the girls of the country.

When the servant came to their house, the two sisters did all they could to get a foot into it, but they could not manage. Cinderilla watched their efforts, and then she said, "May I please try on the slipper?" And her sisters burst out laughing, and began to tease her.

Then the gentleman in charge of the slipper made her sit down, and as he held it to her foot, he found that the shoe slipped on very easily, just as if it had been made of wax. She pulled the other one out of her pocket and put it on, and that is when the fairy appeared again. Now she made Cinderilla's ragged clothes look even more splendid than they had at the palace. When her two sisters realized that she was the lady they had seen at the ball, they threw themselves at her feet, and begged pardon for all the times they had been so cruel. And Cinderilla, who was as kind as she was lovely, married the prince that very day. Then she invited her two sisters to live in the palace, where they married two lords themselves, and they all lived happily together.

Story Number Three

Aschenputtel

Once upon a time, a rich man's wife was very sick. When she felt that her end was near, she called her only daughter to her bedside and said, "Dear child, be good and pious. Then the Dear Lord shall always assist you, and I shall look down from heaven and take care of you." With that, she closed her eyes and died.

The child did as her mother asked, and tried very hard to be good. When winter came, snow covered the earth like a little white blanket. When spring came her father married for the second time.

This stepmother had two daughters of her own, whose faces were pretty but whose hearts were ugly and cold. Times soon grew very bad for the poor stepchild.

"Is the stupid goose to sit in the parlor with us?" said the stepsisters. "Whoever wants to eat bread must earn it." So she was put to work like a servant, getting up before daybreak to bring water, light the fires, and start the cooking and washing. The sisters did everything they could to annoy her.

They jeered at her, and poured peas and lentils into the ashes so that she had to sit there picking them out. At night, when she was tired out with work, she had no bed to sleep in but had to lie in the ashes by the hearth. They started calling her Aschenputtel, or Cinderella, because she always looked dusty and dirty. The dreary days passed, and things went on like this for months, and then years. One day Aschenputtel's father was going to the fair. He asked what each girl wanted him to bring back.

"Dresses of satin!" said the older.

"Diamonds and pearls!" demanded his younger stepdaughter.

But when he asked Aschenputtel what she wanted, she said, "Just break off the first twig which brushes against your hat on the way home, and bring it to me."

So her father went to the fair and brought back two beautiful dresses for the older girl, and pearls and diamonds for the younger. For Aschenputtel, he brought back a hazel branch. She thanked him and took it to her mother's grave in the garden, where she planted it.

Thoughts of her mother filled her mind and she cried so hard that her tears watered the branch. It grew and became a beautiful tree. Three times a day Aschenputtel went to the tree and wept. Each time a little white bird came and perched on the tree and when Aschenputtel made a wish the little bird threw down what she had wished for. In this way, the girl had plenty of food and warm clothing.

One day, the king announced that there would be a royal celebration three days long. All of the unmarried girls of the kingdom were invited, and the prince would pick his bride from among them. Such exciting news!

All three girls danced with excitement, but the stepmother said to Aschenputtel, "You, Aschenputtel? You are all dusty and dirty and yet you want to go to the celebration? How can you go dancing when you've got no clothes or shoes?"

Aschenputtel begged so hard to go that her stepmother said, "Here, I've dumped a bowlful of lentils in the ashes. If you can pick them out in two hours, you may go."

So Aschenputtel went out to the garden and called,

"Oh you tame pigeons, you turtledoves,
and all you birds under heaven,
come and help me pick
The good ones for the little pot,
The bad ones for your little crop!"

Birds of all kinds fluttered down and in less than an hour they had pecked the good lentils into the pot and eaten the bad ones.

When the girl ran to tell her stepmother, the woman broke her promise. She said, "No, Aschenputtel, you don't have any clothes, nor do you know how to dance. Everyone would only laugh at you."

But her stepdaughter begged so hard that she said, "If you can pick two bowlfuls of lentils out of the ashes in one hour I'll let you come along."

So Aschenputtel called again for the birds, and they came and once more put the bad lentils in their crops and the good ones into the pot.

And once again, the stepmother broke her promise. When she saw the bowls full of lentils she said, "We'd only be ashamed of you." Then she turned her back and hurried away with her own two daughters.

After they left, Aschenputtel went to her mother's grave. She stood under the hazel tree and called out,

"Shake and wobble, little tree!
Let gold and silver fall all over me!"

So the bird tossed down a gold and silver dress and slippers embroidered with silk and silver. Aschenputtel changed into the fine dress and slippers, and ran to the palace. Nobody recognized her, not even her stepmother and stepsisters. They were so sure that Aschenputtel would be picking lentils out of the fireplace all night that they did not think it was possible for her to be present.

All evening the king's son danced with the lovely stranger. Whenever someone came and asked her to dance, he said, "She is my partner."

But suddenly, the girl wanted to go home. He offered to escort her because he wanted to find out what her family was like. But she did not want him to see. She got away from him and hid in her father's dovecote, a cage for his birds.

The king's son waited until Aschenputtel's father arrived. Then he told him that he had seen a strange girl run into the dovecote. So the father got an ax and chopped it to pieces but there was no one inside.

When the stepmother and her daughters came home, Aschenputtel was lying in the ashes in her filthy clothes. She had sneaked out the back end of the dovecote and run to the hazel tree, where she had taken off her gold and silver dress. The bird had taken them away. Then she had put on her old, gray dress again, and crept into the kitchen, where she sat down in front of the fire.

The next day all was repeated. The older girls mocked their young stepsister, and their mother called her foul names. Aschenputtel cried, and her family left her home alone.

Once again she called to the bird and this time it threw down a dress that was even more dazzling that the first. She ran to the palace and danced with the king's son, and when he asked if he could escort her home, she ran away. Behind her house there was a garden, where a large tree grew. It had the most wonderful pears growing on it, and Aschenputtel climbed among the branches as nimbly as a squirrel. The king's son didn't know what had become of her, so he waited until her father came out and asked him to chop the pear tree down.

The man did this, but there was nobody in it: Aschenputtel had slid down the other side and run home. Again she was curled up on the hearth when her sisters got home, and again made a show of begging to go to the ball the following night. But her stepmother just laughed at her and said, "You? At the palace? Why, the very idea!"

For the third evening, Aschenputtel called to the bird. This time it threw down a dress that sparkled with diamonds, and was more radiant than either of the others. There was also a pair of slippers of pure gold. When she appeared at the palace this night, the people were too amazed to speak. The king's son danced with no one but her, and when someone else asked her for a dance, he said, "She is my partner."

This night she left early, and escaped without a trace. Or so she thought. But the king's son had played a trick on her. He asked his servants to brush the whole staircase with sticky, black pitch. As the girl ran down the stairs, the pitch pulled her left slipper off. The servants picked it up, and brought the delicate, gold shoe to the prince.

He declared, "No one else shall be my wife but the maiden whose foot fits this golden shoe."

The very next day he began to search for her. When he arrived at Aschenputtel's house, her oldest sister was the first to try it on. She took it into the kitchen where no one could see her. But her mother was there and saw that the shoe did not fit. It was too small and the girl couldn't get her big toe in.

So her mother handed her a knife and said, "Cut your toe off. Once you become queen you won't have to walk anymore."

And the girl cut her toe off and forced her foot into the shoe. She gritted her teeth against the pain and went out to the king's son. He smiled when he saw the young lady wearing the shoe, and helped her onto his horse. But as they rode past the grave the two doves were sitting on the hazel tree. They cried out,

"Looky, look, look,
At the shoe that she took,
There's blood all over and the shoe's too small,
She's not the bride you met at the ball."

When the prince looked down and saw the blood oozing out, he brought her home again and asked to try the shoe on the other girl. This time the younger sister took her turn, and again her mother took the girl into the kitchen. This sister got her toes into the shoe but her heel was too big.

So her mother handed her a knife and said, "Cut off a piece of your heel. Once you become queen you won't have to walk anymore."

That is what her daughter did. Then she hobbled out to meet the prince. At first he was fooled, and helped her to climb up on his horse. But as they passed the hazel tree the doves sang out again. Looking at the girl behind him he saw that blood had stained her white stockings red.

He took the girl with the bleeding foot right back home and asked Aschenputtel's father if he was sure that he didn't have one more daughter?

"Well, only dirty little Aschenputtel, a girl that my dead wife left me. She couldn't possibly be the one you seek."

Nevertheless, the prince insisted that every girl be allowed to try. So Aschenputtel quickly washed her face and came out to meet him. He handed her the golden slipper, and of course it fitted her foot perfectly.

"This is my true bride!" exclaimed the prince.

But the stepmother and the two stepsisters were horrified and turned pale with rage. The prince ignored them and took Aschenputtel onto his horse. As they passed the hazel tree the doves called out,

"Looky, look, look,
At the shoe that she took.
The shoe's just right and there's no blood at all,
She's truly the bride that you met at the ball."

So Aschenputtel and the king's son were married. On the wedding day, the doves sat upon her shoulders, one on the right, the other on the left. The stepsisters tried to pretend that they had always been kind to her, and tried to impress the prince. On the way to church the older sister walked on Aschenputtel's right side, and the younger one on the left. The doves came along and pecked out one eye from each of them. On the way back, the stepsisters switched places, and the doves pecked out the other eye from each sister, to punish them for their wickedness and malice.

Catskins

Once upon a time, away up in the mountains in North Carolina, there lived a girl with no father and mother. She stayed with some rich folks and they made her work for her bread. They never paid her any money, didn't even give her clothes. She only had an old dress, and when it was worn ragged, she had no cloth to patch it with. The only thing she could do was patch it with a bunch of old cat skins. Finally, her whole dress was nothing but catskins, tails and all. That is how Catskins got her name.

One day, the rich woman took sick and died. A few days later, Catskins took a bath and put on the dead woman's wedding dress. Then she went out in the yard and walked all over, until the man noticed. He came running! He looked at his servant girl, and she reminded him of his wife so much that he said, "Will you marry me?"

Catskins said, "Yes—if you get me a dress the color of all the fish in all the seas."

He got the dress right away, and asked her again.

And she said, "Yes—if you get me a dress the color of all the birds that fly in the air."

So the man went shopping and bought that kind of dress for her, and came back. He asked the question for the third time.

And now Catskins said, "I will marry you—if you get me a dress the color of all of the leaves in the world."

And the man got that dress, and said, "Now will you marry me?"

"I might marry you," she said to him, "if you'll give me your flying box."

Well, his flying box was a real treasure, the most valuable thing he owned. Yet he longed to marry Catskins, so he gave her the box.

"Now, let's get married!" he said.

So she told him to go out of the room so that she could change into one of her new dresses. He went out the front door, and she took the flying box and carried it out the back door! Then she put all of her dresses into it, hopped in after them and said, "Rise and fly! Way up high!"

The box followed her orders, and she flew away, lickety-split! Pretty soon, she saw a large house with a garden below them. Now she ordered the box, "Light me down, right to the ground." It did that, and she got out. Then she chanted again, "Sink and lock under this rock!"

Then the box sunk down under the rock, and Catskins went on to the large house wearing her catskin dress. The king lived there, so she asked for work in the kitchen. But the cook said, "Do you think I'd hire a thing like you?"

Then the cook's daughter said, "Poor li'l thing, let's give her a chance." So Catskins was allowed to come in and work.

But Cook said, "I'm not eating the food that girl cooks!"

And when Catskins went down to the kitchen in her outlandish clothing, all of the kitchen maids were so scared they ran away! Some came back and peeped around the doors, and shouted, "Scat!' because they thought she was a big cat. Then they saw that it was just a girl wearing cat skins, not some kind of animal, and they laughed.

One night the servants found out that there would be a fancy dance upstairs. Catskins was helping Cook's daughter get ready to go, because she had been invited. That girl was nice, and told her that it would be alright for Catskins to watch the people in their fine clothes come in.

Catskins said she didn't want to go, and acted like she didn't care. But when she was alone again, she snuck out to her rock and chanted, "Rise again and let me in!"

And the box came up and she opened it, and changed into her dress the color of all the fishes.

She went on in to the dance and everybody said, "Who's that?" and, "Who can that be?" when they saw her. But nobody knew.

Well, the king's son noticed Catskins, and danced with her all evening. And right in the middle of the square dancing, while they were doing a step called Lady 'Round the Lady, Catskins ran away. She went straight to her box and flew on back home, and changed into her catskin dress again.

When she got home, the cook's girl asked if Catskins had been to the party. Catskins said she had.

"Did you see the pretty girl?"

"Yes," she said, she had seen that pretty girl.

Then cook's daughter told Catskins not to wake her up until three o'clock the next day. She gave her permission to go and peep again, but Catskins told her, "No thanks."

The next day at three o'clock, she woke up the cook's daughter and helped her change for the dance. Then she sneaked off and changed into the dress that was colored like all the birds of the sky, and went to the dance.

This time she snuck away from the king's son while they were dancing the Virginia Reel. She flew home in her magic box and changed back into her catskin dress.

Later that night, the cook's girl asked if she had been to watch the dancing.

"I sure did go and see it!" laughed Catskins.

"Did you see that pretty girl with the dress the color of birds?"

Catskins said she had.

"Don't you wake me up till four o'clock tomorrow, because I want to be real beautiful," the cook's daughter said. So Catskins let her sleep.

That evening, as the cook's daughter was getting ready for the dance, she said, "If you want to go, I'll lend you one of my dresses, and you can come on in and dance."

And Catskins could not tell her no, so she

thanked her for the dress, and put it on. But as soon as the girl was gone, Catskins went to her secret flying box and changed into her dress of leaf-colors.

For the third night in a row the king's son danced with her all evening. He couldn't keep his hands off her! They danced and danced every single dance, and just before midnight, he grabbed her finger and slid a ring onto it! Well, Catskins took one look at that ring and ran away! And oh! How sad that poor young man became. He took sick the very next day, and the doctors said they couldn't do a thing for him. It was love-sickness, they told the Queen, and the only cure would be to find the girl that the prince had fallen in love with. Meanwhile, the prince must eat.

Well, every one of the girls in town brought food to tempt him. They baked pound cakes and lattice-topped pies, and Cook's daughter made him a tart. The queen took them all to her son's sick-bed, but he refused to eat anything.

One day Catskins said she'd like to bake a cake for the king's son, since everyone else had. "You must be joking!" the old Cook squawked. "You bake him a cake! If he wasn't sick already, he would be by the time he finished any cake you bake."

But cook's daughter said, "Aw, Mama, don't be so mean. Where's the harm of her baking him a cake if she wants to?"

So Catskins baked a cake, and then went and got the ring the king's son had put on her finger, and baked it right into that cake. She made the cake look as pretty as she could, and put white frosting on top. But then the Cook came and took it away from her, and said that she would take the cake upstairs herself. When the queen cut a piece for her son, out fell the ring! What a surprise!

"Why look! It's a ring!" she said.

Now everybody spoke at once, wondering where that ring had come from and who had baked that cake.

"I did," said the old Cook. "I baked that cake myself!"

"You did no such thing!" the king's son told her. "But you had better bring whoever baked that cake here right now, or I'll have your head cut off!"

So the old woman had to go and fetch Catskins. As soon as the young man saw her, he knew that she was the right girl. He smiled at her—and she ran away again!

This time she went back to her flying box and got in, then said, " Rise and fly! Not too high!" so the box took her back to the palace. Quickly, she changed into the dress the color of all the fishes of the sea and ran upstairs.

But the prince said, "No—the other dress!"

So Catskins went and changed into the one the color of all the birds in the sky. And the prince said, "No—that's not right either." So she put on her leaf colored dress and came back in for the third time, and the prince kissed her.

"Will you marry me?" he asked, and Catskins said, "Yes!" So they got married, and they lived long and happy. But some folks say that the king made Cook wear the old catskin dress for the rest of her days.

Chinye

Once upon a time, in Kenya, there lived a girl named Chinye. Her mother had died, and her father remarried. Her stepmother, however, did not have a drop of human kindness. Instead of helping to take care of Chinye, the motherless child, the woman used her to do all of the hardest chores. Because Chinye looked so much like her mother, this stepmother secretly wanted to get rid of her. She began sending her out for water each night. The forest near their home was thick and dark, even during the daytime. At night, it was as black as soot, and filled with the sounds of many animals. Despite her stepdaughter's protests, the cruel second wife forced her out into the night.

"And don't come back with an empty gourd!" she shouted, "or you know what will happen."

So Chinye had to go out into the dark woods. She crept slowly along, feeling her way before her. Suddenly, she heard a growl and felt something large rush past her! It was a cheetah racing by and Chinye shook with fright. Yet she crept onwards.

Soon, she heard snorting and snuffling. It was a herd of wildebeests settling down for the night. Chinye tiptoed past them, and walked on towards the lake. At last, she could smell the water. Quietly she moved towards the rippling water. Then she froze: there was a pride of lions drinking! Now Chinye was really afraid. If she stepped forward to fill her gourds, the lions would eat her. But if she went home without the water, her stepmother would beat her. As she stood shivering behind a tree, she felt something touch her head. She looked up and saw that there was a large pink bird standing next to her!

"What are you doing here, my child?" the flamingo asked her.

"I have come to fill my water gourd, but I am afraid of the lions."

"You would be a fool if you were not afraid of the lions," answered the flamingo solemnly. Then it said, "I will take care of the lions. When you hear me call once, be ready. When you hear me call twice, fill your gourd. And when you hear me call three times, run as fast as you can!"

So Chinye waited by the lake until she heard the flamingo call once. She held her gourd tightly, and looked over at the lions. They had all turned toward the sound of the bird. Now the flamingo called for the second time. Quick as a flash, Chinye darted forward and filled her gourd. Just as the water filled it, Chinye heard the flamingo call for the third time. She ran as fast as she could! Now she heard laughter, and realized that the flamingo was hopping through the trees just ahead of her.

"This way, Chinye! Come this way!"

So Chinye followed the flamingo, and suddenly, there before her, she saw a hut. She had never seen a hut near the lake before, and wondered how it came to be there. An old woman stood in the doorway, and beckoned to her.

When Chinye came near, the woman said, "Chinye, my daughter, you are an old and worthy soul. You should be living a good life now, not suffering at the hands of your stepmother. Come, child. Come in to my hut."

So Chinye came into the hut. "Sweep the floor for an old woman, now, for my bones are stiff and I cannot draw the broom." So Chinye carefully set her water gourd down, took up a palm broom, and began to sweep the floor. She saw that it was entirely covered with gourds! Some were very small, and others were huge, and they were of all colors.

"How will I sweep the floor, Grandmother? It is all covered with gourds," asked the girl.

And the old one said, "You must bend and pick up the tiniest gourds, those no bigger than your thumb."

But when Chinye bent to the floor, the big gourds pushed in front of the little gourds, and called out, "Take me! Take me!"

Calmly, Chinye pushed the big gourds aside and gathered the small ones. When her apron was full of them, she said, "What shall I do now, Grandmother?"

And the old one said, "You must tie them up in your apron and take them home. When you get there, crack them open, and see what happens!"

So Chinye tied her apron corners together to make a bag, and filled it with the little gourds. Then she picked up her water gourd and went home following the laughing flamingo.

When she got home, her stepmother stormed and shouted. "Why were you gone so long? Were you playing in the lake? You lazy good-for-nothing, I shall beat you if that gourd is not filled to the brim!"

And Chinye gave her the water gourd, and showed her that it was filled to the brim. Then she said, "Stepmother, please excuse me for being late. There was an old woman in the woods and I swept her floor for her and she has given me gourds."

With that, Chinye drew out a handful of gourds. She cracked them open, and her stepmother's eyes nearly popped out of her face. From each gourd spilled pearls, and rubies, and emeralds! She grabbed as many of these as she could, so quickly that Chinye did not have time to pick any of them up. Then she made the girl tell her exactly what she had done, and where the woman's hut was. So Chinye told her, and the woman made her own daughter take an empty water gourd and go to the lake. The girl quaked and shivered in the woods just as Chinye had done.

When she got to the lake, the lions were still there, and so was the flamingo. The big pink bird told her to be ready when it called once, to fill the jug when it called twice, and to run like the wind when it called the third time. This Chinye's stepsister did, and soon her gourd was filled to the brim.

In two steps she reached the hut of the old woman. This one beckoned for her to come in, and the girl rushed over. When the old woman asked her to sweep the floor, she set her gourd on the table, and grabbed the broom. But when she tried to sweep, she saw that the entire floor was covered with gourds.

"How shall I sweep, old woman? Your floor is dirty with gourds."

And the old woman told her to gather the tiniest ones, and leave the big ones alone. And Chinye's stepsister bent forward, and the big gourds jumped up and down calling out to her. The little gourds lay quietly on the floor. The greedy girl laughed aloud and grabbed four of the biggest gourds she could carry. Without even bothering to pick up her water gourd, she ran home.

Her mother was there, waiting to see what she would bring. "Open them up!" urged the woman, and she grabbed two of the calabashes from her daughter. Each took a knife and sliced the big rinds open. And then what a wailing Chinye heard! Those big gourds were filled with wasps and biting flies and scorpions. They swarmed and bit every inch of Chinye's stepmother and sister, but they didn't touch Chinye herself.

Now those two wicked women began to swell up, their faces turning red and their eyes running. They scratched and slapped at themselves in their attempts to get the bugs off, and ripped off their clothing, so frantic were they. All of the villagers gathered around and laughed and laughed at the two naked women, covered with bee stings and hornet bites. The stepmother and her daughter ran, and Chinye's father ran after them. And the last time I looked, they were still running.

As for Chinye, she went back to the hut and cut open the rest of the little gourds. There were enough jewels there to make a thousand women rich, so Chinye invited all of the women of the village to come with her to sell the jewels in town. With the money, they bought large herds of cattle, goats and pigs, and Chinye and the sisters of her village lived in peace and plenty for many years.

Section Two

Symbolism of Commonly Found Animals and Objects in the World-Wide Cinderella Story

Part One
Birds as Helpers

The scientific classification *Aves* covers a gigantic group of warm-blooded winged animals called birds. It is divided into twenty-eight orders and one hundred fifty-eight families, covering thousands of species of birds. They are found in every country of the world.

Birds have fascinated humans at least since the first cave paintings. Some of the earliest of these human paintings, including those in Lascaux, France, show shamans in bird masks. The early mythologies of humankind depict birds in the Cosmic Tree, as in the Norse legend of Yggdrasil, the gigantic ash tree that supports the universe. Ancient Egyptians depicted their god, Thoth, with the head of bird, pointing to his role as judge and transcendent figure.

One of the earliest characterizations of birds is the Phoenix. In legend, it lives five hundred years, then uses its last modicum of vitality to build itself a "nest of spice branches" upon which to immolate itself. The phoenix is born anew from the ashes, thus making the bird a symbol of rebirth, as well as of the sun. In Christian tradition the Phoenix is recognized as a metaphor for the son of God, while in Chinese and Japanese lore that bird was one of a quaternity of sacred animals.

Birds are mysterious and enviable creatures to earth-bound human beings. Their ability to traverse the air, to fly across the sky—the domain of the gods—makes them mystical in many cultures and divine in others. They can be messengers from heaven sent to communicate with people, or they can carry up messages from earth. The Teutonic figure of Odin was kept informed of human doings by two ravens that sat upon his shoulders. The ancient Greeks viewed the raven as an oracle of Apollo.

Christian angels, with their feathered wings, are cousin to birds. When the prophet Ezekiel was visited by the four cherubim, he described their physical form as "like that of a man but each of them had four faces and four wings." The sound made by their sixteen rushing wings roared "like waters, like the voice of the Almighty." In Genesis, after Noah had been afloat for the days and nights of the flood, he sent two birds in search of land.

For the Apache Indians of North America, Big Owl was evoked as a man-eating ogre. Ancient Egyptians used the image of a person's head on a bird's body to show the soul of a dead person, demonstrating that the bird was seen by them as the "separable soul" of a person. In the Philippines, bird-men called *alans* figure as tricksters and mischief makers, usually benevolent toward human beings.

Birds can represent the elements of the psychic self that are intuitive and creative. The movement of birds, whether soaring through the air or stepping nimbly across the grass, is evocative of the inspiration of an idea. Ideas can come to one from a source apparently unconnected to the problem at hand, seeming to swoop across vast stretches of space. Birds can flutter away unexpectedly, with little provocation, as can inspiration.

Many birds are small, as children are, which is perhaps why they are one of the oldest and most common helper animals and friends of children in literature. Fairy tales are filled with birds as companions, assistants, and spies, quite likely because they were such a ubiquitous part of life. Birds' eggs of all kinds are obvious images of the life cycle.

In the story of *The Second Voyage of Sinbad the Seaman*, told by Scheherazade in *The Arabian Nights*, Sinbad saves himself by means of a gigantic egg. Stranded on an island, he climbs a tree and sees in the distance "a huge white dome rising in the air, and of vast compass." Sinbad binds himself to the egg, and when the enormous mother Rukh returns, she carries egg and man away:

> As soon as the dawn broke and the morn shone, the Rukh rose off its egg and spreading its wings with a great cry flew up into the air dragging me with it; nor ceased it to soar and to tower till I thought it had reached the limit of the firmament...

Charles Perrault's *Histoire ou contes du temps passé de ma mere l'Oye* , or *Stories and Tales of Times Past and Mother Goose Tales,* first published in French in 1697, continued the tradition of birds in literature, casting an old granny on a gigantic flying goose as the bearer of his rhymes. An update of Perrault's short verses done two hundred years later still feels relevant. Published as *The Real Mother Goose* and edited in 1916 by Mary Hill Arbuthnot, the book is a classic of children's literature in the English language. In 2013 it is still widely available in many formats.

Goosey-Goosey Gander and his wanderings, the cock who crows, "Cock-a-doodle do, my dame has lost her shoe!" and the *Song of Sixpence*, are well-known examples. That verse celebrates "four and twenty blackbirds, baked in a pie" as a "dainty dish to set before the king," reminding us that birds, above all else, have been an important food source throughout history.

Birds appear in most Cinderella stories, in one role or another. They help her to sort peas from ashes, sesame seeds from maize, or bring her fine clothing. In one Indian version, Bopaluchi, it is the birds of the forest that alert the girl her uncle is false and means her harm. In the German story of *Aschenputtel*, as well as in *The Golden Sandal*, a story from Iraq, it is a bird who warns the prince that he has been tricked with the wrong bride. A crow warns the Iraqi prince, while white pigeons alert the Hessian the Grimms described. In the Egyptian Cinderella, Rhodopis, a slave girl has been given slippers of "rose red gold" by her master. A falcon, symbolizing the god Horus, swoops down from the sky and snatches one shoe, dropping it into the Pharoah's garden and triggering a search for the girl with the slipper's mate. In one ancient story from Vietnam, Cinderella herself is turned into first a golden turtle and then a bamboo shoot, before becoming a little bird.

Modern American culture continues to feature birds in a strong role as children's playmates and guides. The ubiquitous bath-time rubber ducky is one incarnation of this powerful animal archetype, demonstrating the enduring influence such images continue to have on human beings. Donald Duck, originally drawn by artists Art Babbitt and Dick Huemer in 1934, went on to become a Disney staple, recognized by children all over the world. A little yellow chick called Tweety Bird, dreamed up by Looney Tunes in 1954, taps into the archetypal bird, as do the marshmallow candies known as Peeps. The quintessential American bird friend still with us in the 21st century is Big Bird, from the Children's Television Workshop show for preschoolers, *Sesame Street*.

Chickens (*Gallus domesticus*) are symbolically connected to dawn and rebirth. Roosters, since they crow to announce the dawn, seemed to the superstitious to actually bring about the daylight. Sleeping puts one in a state of vulnerability, and roosters are often believed to keep watch over people while they sleep. The rooster is the traditional image on weather vanes, because of the belief that roosters keep watch over the churches and houses upon whose roofs they sit.

A form of divination practiced in ancient Rome used a white cock, the alphabet, and dried corn kernels. After a circle was drawn on the ground, the letters of the alphabet were then inscribed around the perimeter, a kernel placed upon each one. A white cock was let loose in the center of the circle and the order in which it pecked the letters carefully transcribed.

Crows (Corvus brachyrynchos) are found in Europe as well as Asia and North America. They have been connected with bad news for thousands of years. The crow was a familiar of the Greek Goddess Athena, and it was a crow that carried ill tidings to her about the death of her baby. The existence of the child Erichthonius, who was born with a serpent's tail, was supposed to have been kept secret. Athena gave him to King Cecrops to foster, but the baby fell to its death from a precipice, as did the little princesses who had been playing with the serpent-boy. The crow who saw it flew straight to Athena with the news. She was so shocked that she dropped the stone cuttings meant for the construction of her temple, the Acropolis. In rage and grief, she turned the bird's feathers from white to black.

In both European and American folk culture, crows bring bad luck. A traditional poem tells the meaning behind a flock of crows:

One for sorrow,
Two for mirth,

Three for a wedding,
Four for a birth,
Five for silver,
Six for gold,
Seven for a secret not to be told,
Eight for heaven,
Nine for hell,
And ten for the devil's very own self.

Crows appear as tricksters in American Indian mythology. They are known to be resourceful, as the Aesop's Fable *The Crow and the Pitcher* demonstrates. Here the crafty bird cannot reach water at the bottom of a pitcher. It then drops pebbles in to raise the level of the water, thus quenching its thirst and yielding the moral, "Necessity is the mother of invention." A Cinderella story from Finland features a gown made entirely from crow skins.

Ducks are members of the order Anseriformes, which also includes swans and geese. These are social birds, often swimming in family groups; thus, they represent unity and filial loyalty. In the original Brothers Grimm story of *Hansel and Gretel*, it is a duck that carries them over a lake to get back home to their father.

Famous ducks in literature and song include folk singer Burl Ives' rendition of *The Little White Duck,* who is "swimming in the water, doing what he ought'er, saying Quack, Quack, Quack!" Robert McCloskey's classic children's story of ducks in urban Boston, *Make Way for Ducklings* (1941) illustrates the love of a mother duck for her brood.

Cinderella and other fairy tale characters are often put to work as poultry herders, as in *The Goose Girl*. Sometimes ducklings are not ducklings at all, as in Hans Christian Anderson's tale of *The Ugly Duckling*.

Doves, all three hundred species of them, are members of the order *Columbiformes*. White doves are a symbol of peace, purity, innocence, and love, especially between marriage partners. Doves can also be emblems of sexuality, as shown by Ishtar, the Babylonian Goddess of love and war. This meaning was also important to African slaves transported to the United States, who believed dove's hearts to be a sort of edible love charm. The dove can symbolize a soul bound for Heaven or the Holy Ghost. In the Bible, it is a dove that returns to bring Noah a twig after being released, proving that there is land nearby.

The mourning dove, *Zenaida macroura*, and the turtledove, *Streptopelia turtus*, are most common in Cinderella stories. The 1812 story *Aschenputtel*, or Cinderella, collected by the Brothers Grimm, features pigeons, members of the dove family, taking vengeance on Cinderella's stepsisters by pecking out their eyes.

Owls, including the Great Horned Owl, *Bubo virginianus,* are symbolic of wisdom, strength, or death, depending upon the belief system followed. The owl is one of the forms taken by Athena, the Greek goddess of wisdom and war. The beautiful, fine-boned Burrowing Owl, *Athene cunicularia*, is named for her. In Celtic legend the owl was known as the "corpse bird" because of its nighttime hunting. The Romans interpreted the hoot of an owl as an omen of impending death. In pre-Columbian North America, as well as Egypt, owls were also associated with death. Pima American Indians thought the owl to be the embodiment of a departed soul. Medieval Europeans were certain that owls, afoot at night when decent creatures sleep, were minions of the Devil.

Some American Indians took a different view of owls, honoring them for their ability to hunt in the dark. In India, the eyeballs of an owl are sometimes eaten for their sympathetic powers of strong eyesight. Because owls are nocturnal they are associated with the nighttime, and thus with the moon. Nineteenth-century poet Edward Lear may have been aware of this connection when he wrote about the "elegant fowl." His 1871 poem, *The Owl and the Pussy Cat*, concludes with the bridal couple under the moon's glow:

> And hand in hand, on the edge of the sand,
> they danced by the light of the moon,
> the moon, the moon,
> they danced by the light of the moon.

Lunar thoughts, which can be *lunatic*, or unusual, often spring from deep within the unconscious mind. Such ideas may come forth in dreams and be only partially remembered, or dimly illuminated, unlike thoughts conceived during the day under the bright light of the sun. In popular American culture, the Wise Old Owl is iconic of the studious, learned intellectual. The owl that guides baby animals in the Walt Disney classic film *Bambi* is an example.

Owls appear often in children's literature. A prominent figure in A. A. Milne's *Winnie the Pooh* is Owl, or Wol as he spells it, who does his best to be the smartest animal in the Forty Acre Woods.

In 1953 it was a "parliament of owls" led by the wise Glimfeather who assisted young Jill and Eustace in their fight against evil in the *The Silver Chair,* Book Four of the *Narnia Series* by C.S. Lewis. The twentieth-century blockbuster *Harry Potter* series continues this tradition with boy-wizard Harry and his companion and messenger, Hedwig the Owl.

Ravens, or *Corvus corax,* are often seen as messengers of the gods. The prophet Elijah was fed by a raven during his exile in the wilderness while his country was being punished by God for idolatry. They are guardians in some African cultures. In fairy tales they are often transformed people, perhaps because of their large size. In Europe and India they are bad-luck creatures, associated with death. Edgar Allen Poe certainly felt that way. His 1845 poem *The Raven,* immortalized this connection with the stanza:

> Ghastly, grim and ancient Raven
>> wandering from the Nightly shore—
> Tell me what thy lordly name
>> is on the Night's Plutonium Shore!
> Quoth the Raven, "Nevermore."

Turkeys. It has been confirmed that wild turkeys, *Melleagris gallopavo*, have been present in North America since at least the 1st century C.E. Spanish missionaries who observed the Zuni and Anasazi people recorded their use of turkey feathers in elaborately made headdresses. Due to their large size and hollow bone structure, turkey bones were used to make tubular containers, beads, and a variety of other household objects.

Their feathers were of ceremonial importance, used in precise ways in the making of prayer sticks. Offered to the gods at both summer and winter solstice, as well as at other selected times, the sacred items required a variety of feathers. The number and type on each stick depended upon which individual family member it was being made for. Women had two feathers from a turkey to represent their forefathers, as well as a downy turkey feather for the self, and a downy eagle feather, representing the moon. Men got four turkey feathers, one of which represented the sun. These feathers were followed in sequence by others, including those of ducks, blue jays, and robins. Pueblo people of prehistory kept domesticated turkeys, and probably used them as a food source as well as for their plumage.

Turkeys were of great value to this culture, used as food as well as in ceremony. An American Indian Cinderella story, *The Poor Turkey Girl*, is one of the few that does not have a happy ending. In this story, the girl commits a serious offense by neglecting her flock, which has provided her with finery to attend a celebration. They abandon her, leaving her without their eggs, feathers, and her own livelihood.

Woodpeckers (Melanerpes) are a group of 210 species, including *picoides pubescens*, common all over North America. These busy little workers, with their distinctive rat-a-tat-tat pecking, build nests in cooperative communities. Woodpeckers' cheerful pecking can sound companionable to humans, making them obvious fairy tale helpers. Since both males and females sit on their eggs, this may explain their reputation as "family birds." Their small size and industriousness make them appealing friends for children, as well as role models of loyalty. Woodpecker appears in this capacity in one of the Jataka Tales told about the life of Siddhartha Gautama Buddha.

In the story, *Three Friends in a Forest*, Buddha is incarnated as a golden antelope. At the shores of the lake he meets a green turtle and a woodpecker, and they form the habit of conversation each day. One day a hunter lays a snare, and the golden antelope is caught fast. His friend Woodpecker comes to soothe him, counseling him to remain calm, lest his struggles tighten the snare further. Turtle comes and gnaws through the leather snare, and the golden antelope bounds away. But Woodpecker knows that the hunter will come out of his hut at the noise, and flies into his face when the door opens. Woodpecker won't let the hunter out the front door, so the man goes around to the back door. Wise Woodpecker is one step ahead of him, and delays the hunter long enough for Buddha to escape.

The character of Woody Woodpecker, inspired by a real-life woodpecker in 1940, offered comic relief and a touch of friendly zaniness during the troubling times of World War Two.

Part Two
More Animal Helpers

Cats

Of the family *Felidae,* genus *Felis,* house cats, *F. domesticus,* have a long history as companions of human beings, for both practical and spiritual reasons. Since mice have likely been nibbling from human food sources for as long as humans have stored food, it would seem that cats have been hunting mice in human habitations all that time.

Cats, as anyone who has ever observed one knows, are baffling and mysterious creatures. They can be silent and swift and can see at night. Thus they can be seen as evocative of death and darkness. A cat crossing one's path is considered an ill omen, while a cat seen washing its face can be a predictor of rain.

In ancient Egyptian mythology Bastet was a cat goddess who guarded mankind and provided for its prosperity. For this reason, cats were seen as sacred animals. Their images can still be seen in the necropolis Beni Hassan. In European folklore, cats are associated with the Devil; therefore, harming a cat can bring bad luck. In Buddhist tradition, the cat was one of two animals that was aloof to the death of Buddha.

The Japanese have a devotion to the benevolent cat spirit of legend, Tama. Originally, he was the cherished pet of Lady Usugumo of Tokyo, for whose sake Tama gave his life. He was slain by a visitor who was frightened at the cat's snarling. But after Tama's head was cut off, it flew up to the ceiling beams and killed a poisonous snake that had been about to drop onto his mistress. She was inconsolable. To make up for the loss, the visitor commissioned a carved replica of Tama. The lady was soothed and the "beckoning cat" became a totem of health and serenity.

Cats are frequently found in fairy tales, especially in the company of old women. They are often associated with witches, and like witches themselves, they may be good or evil. Baba Yaga, the witch woman of Russian lore, was said to keep a cat. Often their traditional role of mouse hunter is evident as the cat works to hinder the protagonist. They often speak or have human characteristics, as does the remarkable cat given to the miller's youngest son in *Puss In Boots*.

There is a variant of the Cinderella story known as the *Catskin Tale*. In this kind of story, the girl must escape from being forced into a marriage she does not want, often to her father. She begs to be given three very special dresses, promising to marry after she is given each one. When this does not work she stalls for more time by asking for a cloak made from the skins of cats, sometimes black. In other versions the cloak is made from bird feathers or the skins of other animals, but all such tales are known as *Catskin*.

Cats can be nature spirits and often appear as entertainers. An example of this is the Cheshire Cat in Lewis Caroll's *Alice's Adventures in Wonderland (1865)*. Contemporary celebrity cats of literature include Jim Davis' *Garfield* and Dr. Seuss's ground-breaking character, *The Cat in the Hat* (1958). He is still going strong after more than half a century.

Cousin to the house cat is the lion, *Panthera leo*, which is often found in folk tales and fables. Symbols of power though they are, lions are not invincible. Aesop's Fable of *The Lion, The Bear and The Fox*, in which lion and bear fight over a kill which is lost to a sneaky fox, demonstrates an important moral: in many a quarrel, both sides lose.

Lions can be simultaneously frightening and funny, as L. Frank Baum's Cowardly Lion in *The Wizard of Oz* (1900) showed. Or they can be scary, but with a tame side, as in the 1952 picture book classic, *The Tawny Scrawny Lion*. They can be regal, as is the character Aslan from the 1950 C. S. Lewis fantasy, *The Lion, the Witch, and the Wardrobe*. They can be timid, as in Robert Kraus's *Leo the Late Bloomer* (1971). The protagonist is a very timid lion cub, who takes longer than all the others of the den to mature.

Cows

Cattle, oxen and buffalos are ungulates and members of the *Bovid* family. They are ruminating beasts with four stomach chambers, which may explain why they tend to be seen as symbols of plenty. Cows have been friends to humans for many centuries. Their milk is made into cheese in many parts of the world, providing a major source of sustenance. Cows provide milk for children to drink, as do human mothers, thus making them a common mother substitute figure. The cows of yesteryear had curved horns, and these reminded people of the waxing and waning moon. Since the moon is a feminine entity in virtually all cultures, the cow, like the moon, is seen as an archetypal mother image.

The twelve Olympians who were the divine family of the ancient Greeks included Zeus the Great and his wife–and sister–Hera, called Juno by the Romans. Edith Hamilton described her as "the protector of marriage and married women" and noted that Hera has roots in paganism. Hamilton said:

> There are traces of a time when there were beast-gods. The satyrs are goat-men and the centaurs are half man, half horse. Hera is often called 'cow-faced,' as if the adjective had somehow stuck to her through all her changes from divine cow to the very human queen of heaven.

In India the cow is venerated and respected, as Hinduism endows cows with souls. From the sacred cow to the divine cow a line can be drawn from India to Egypt. The ancient Egyptian goddess of the sky, Nut, was sometimes portrayed as a cow.

In the Christian tradition, especially in England and Ireland, it is said that cows can talk on Christmas Eve, but that bad luck will come to any who overhear their speech. The belief comes from the story of the Baby Jesus' birth in an ox's stall. The bovine is said to have kneeled before him, thus making it and all of its kind "blessed animals."

Blood from the cosmic ox Geush Urvan was believed, in Zoroastrianism, to be the source of all life. Ox blood was also a favorite sacrificial offering to the gods of ancient Greece and Rome. The animal's sheer brute strength in the pre-industrial age made it as valuable in plowing fields and drawing wagons as the combustion engine is today.

The Lakota tribe of American Indians holds White Buffalo Woman as one of their most sacred emblems. Their legend tells that after the first people were destroyed in a flood, the second people had not yet learned to venerate the buffalo, and suffered because of it. They hunted the animal, and had some success, but it was via White Buffalo Woman that they learned to communicate with the Great Spirit by sending smoke up to him. As a deity in human form, she taught the people to smoke tobacco while praying, and brought them the Sacred Calf Pipe. She taught them to honor the buffalo, to hunt it, and to use its carcass wisely. The buffalo is a fertility symbol for many American Indian tribes, and thus is associated with children.

The Pious Ox, a story from the Jewish tradition,

tells of a man who was forced by poverty to sell his farm and his ox. The Christian who bought the creature was dismayed to find that it refused to work on the Sabbath. He complained to the previous owner, who explained the reason for the ox's behavior. This caused the buyer to reconsider his own habits of working on that day. The ox is also the symbol of St. Luke, representing his steady patience.

In the Japanese zodiac, those born in the Year of the Ox share its traits of being steady, hard workers, determined in their endeavors.

Cows are popular animals with positive associations. Even in the 21st century, the image of cows as bountiful, benevolent animals persists. Milk and cheese are still important regional products in the United States, and cows have been used as advertising mascots ever since large-scale advertising began in the twentieth century. The Borden Dairy Company chose an especially photogenic cow and named her Elsie for her public debut in the early 1930's. She starred at the company's booth during the 1939 New York World's Fair, and her image is still is use today.

The American lumberjack of tall tales, giant Paul Bunyan, was said to work with an enormous blue ox. As the old loggers told the tale in the first decade of the twentieth century, when Paul was born he weighed over a hundred pounds. Each day for breakfast he ate "five dozen eggs, tens sacks of potatoes, and a half a barrel of mush." It was on Paul's twenty-first birthday that he went out in a snowstorm so cold that the hills, the trees, and even the air had turned blue. He saw something protruding from a snowdrift, gave it a tug, and pulled out "the biggest baby ox on earth." Everything but its curved white horns was as blue as the snow around it. He took the big baby home and nurtured it. The ox thrived, but stayed blue. He named it Babe, and it grew so big that he "had to look through a telescope just to see what Babe's hind legs were doing."

It seems possible that the archetype of the friendly horned Bovid survives in contemporary American culture due, in part, to Babe. *The Story of Ferdinand*, that tender-hearted bull who wanted to relax under a cork tree, smelling the flowers, was written in 1936, and it continues to be a staple of American preschoolers today. Author Munro Leaf portrayed this gentle bull's transformation from petal-sniffer to rampaging monster as being induced by a bee sting. In his story, all of the brave matadors, picadors, and banderilleros sulk and stamp their feet because Ferdinand won't get up and fight. After the bull is stung, the proud men with their red capes and sharp sticks get what they have been waiting for. Yet the story ends with Ferdinand relaxing peacefully under a tree, his sting—and his temper—soothed.

When the Borden Dairy Company added a chemical division during World War Two, it was decided that Elsie the Cow should be reserved for association with food products. The advertising icon Elmer the Bull was therefore created for their new brand of school glue. Today he is recognized by millions of children, his face adorning plastic squeeze bottles and twistable sticks of Elmer's brand adhesive.

In the Chinese Zodiac, those born in the Year of the Ox are said to be patient, reliable, and family oriented. Perhaps the role of Bovids in folk stories is in character with the animal's nature.

In fairy tales cows frequently offer advice, guidance, or magical food and clothing. In many Cinderella stories, Bovids help the girl do her impossible tasks. In fact, the cow is second only to birds as the most popular animal helper. In the Korean Cinderella story of *Pear Blossom*, it is an ox who assists her, while in the Vietnamese *Two Sisters,* a water buffalo helps weed the rice patty. Cows sometimes provide the Cinderella character milk and honey when she is starving, or help after their own death. It is a magic box found in the paunch of the butchered cow that aids in *La Brutta Centenarola*, a Cinderella tale from Italy. Cow's horns are frequently magical containers or musical instruments blown to summon help. In such stories, the cow is believed to represent the girl's dead mother.

Cows in poetry and nursery rhymes are often amusing figures:

> I've never seen a purple cow,
> I never hope to see one.
> But I can tell you anyhow,
> I'd rather see than be one. (Burgess, G. 1915)

Crocodiles and Alligators

The reptilian order *Crocodilia* is an ancient one. It appeared on our planet at least three hundred million years ago. There are four members, including crocodiles and alligators. Both are big amphibious reptiles. The Nile crocodile was at one time common throughout the African continent. The mugger crocodile is native to India and Pakistan. North American crocodiles, *Crocodylus acutus*, are native to the southeastern region of the United States.

Crocodiles are large predators and humans who come into contact with them often become prey. They are seen as cruel and coldblooded in most cultures, and are often associated with death. The ancient Egyptian crocodile god, Sebek, sometimes called Suchos, waited and watched as each soul was weighed. The bad ones were his to devour.

In some locales crocodiles were hunted, while in others they were deified. Crocodilopolis was an Egyptian community temple by a lake. The sacred crocodile who lived there was tended carefully. He was Petasuchsos, said to be Sebek incarnate, and adorned with golden earrings and bracelets on his ankles. His image can be found in the Valley of the Kings at the tomb of Seti Merempath.

The African tribe of Malagasy clans, whose name is translated as "son of crocodile," tells this story:

> There was a woman that lived in a river with a crocodile for her husband. One day another man trapped her to be his own wife. She bore him two sons, then escaped and returned to the

river. Her descendants have been safe from crocodiles ever since.

In Madagascar, something like a collective soul is
believed to accrue in the bodies or body parts of
certain animals. This entity is called a *razane*, and
the souls of departed chiefs were believed to reside
as *razanes* in the teeth of crocodiles. Powerful
amulets were made from them, worked with silver
and beads.

In African-American folk tales originating with
captured slaves brought to the United States, alligator characters replace the crocodile characters featured in their native Africa. In *Bruh Alligator Meets
Trouble*, Br'er Rabbit teaches a gator the meaning
of the word by setting fire to his swamp, causing
his skin to wrinkle and blacken.

In a *Jataka* told about the Buddha, a crocodile
personifies danger, which the Buddha defeats
through bravery and cunning. In that story, Buddha
exists as a monkey who wishes to cross a river for
better fruit. A crocodile offers to take him across,
and the monkey accepts the ride. Midstream, the
croc announces that he will now eat the monkey's
heart. Buddha-Monkey remains calm, tells the
crocodile that he has left his heart hanging from a
tree branch, and points out a fig tree hanging over
the water. When the crocodile swims over to eat the
fig, Buddha-Monkey jumps to safety.

In the sacred Hindu text *The Ramayana*, a crocodile stars in one of many attempts to kill Rama
and his helper, the monkey Hanuman, Son of the
Wind. During one of many extravagant battles fea-

turing hundreds of thousands of chariot-driving demons and their ten-headed king, Ravana, Rama's brother Lakshmana is killed. The divine Hanuman is dispatched to the sacred Gandhamardhan Mountains to gather a particular medicinal flower to revive him.

But he is enticed into the river itself, where lives a notorious female crocodile called Ghandakali, who attacks him. Hanuman's prowess is such that he kills Ghandakali, then shreds her body for good measure. That's when "a bright spirit" arises from its corpse and ascends to the skies. It calls down to Hanuman to thank him for breaking the curse that the god Vishnu had foretold.

Crocodiles appear in Cinderella stories from Indonesia and the Philippines. In both of these instances the character is female. Perhaps the stability of an ancient creature, combined with the nurturing that crocodiles show their young, makes them suitable wise women figures. It may also be an evocation of the female water spirit found in so many cultures, whose role is reminiscent of *Baba Yaga*. This witch woman of Russia, who flies about in a mortar and lives in a moveable hut that walks on chicken legs, is both good and evil. She has iron teeth and sometimes eats children, but at other times helps poor girls in need, at least those who show respect for her. The old woman in the Kenyan Cinderella story of *Chinye* is such a character as well, identifiable by her proximity to the river as well as her request for household help.

In Judy's Sierra's *The Gift of the Crocodile*

(2000), a Cinderella story from the Spice Islands, Grandmother Crocodile provides a silver sarong for the girl to wear after the girl cares for her baby crocodile despite its bad smell and sharp teeth. The beast protects the girl but devours her cruel stepsisters, much like Baba Yaga does.

One of the greatest man-eating crocodiles of English literature lived in Never-Never Land with Peter Pan. During one of the battles between the gang of Lost Boys and the pirate Captain Hook, Peter Pan chopped off the captain's hand and fed it to the crocodile—thus the need for the hook. One taste of pirate was not enough for the gigantic croc, and he trailed the Captain wherever he went. Hook finally tossed him an alarm clock, which the crocodile swallowed whole, forever after announcing his whereabouts with an ominous tick-tock.

Crocodiles of contemporary literature include the picture books Bernard Waber's *Lyle, Lyle Crocodile* (1987), the story of a brave young pet who saves a neighbor from fire. Lyle first appeared in Waber's 1962 book, *The House on 88th St.* Maurice Sendak famously featured gators in his alphabet book, *Alligators All Around*, also published in 1962. This alliterative alphabet book features the beasts in action, "Bursting balloons, catching colds, doing dishes." They are dressed, of course, in smocks, cowboy boots, aprons, and all sorts of other outfits.

Fish

When life first formed on this planet, it happened in the deep blue sea. Fishes have been swimming in the water that covers so much of earth's surface for about 438 million years, and are categorized as either jawed or jawless. There are more than 21,000 species of these vertebrates, and they come in all sizes and colors. They are a major source of global nutrition.

In cultures that venerate age, long-living fish such as carp are symbols of longevity and endurance. This is because carp travel far in their lives, swimming upstream, persevering to fulfill their needs.

Fish have a powerful significance for Christians, as they are symbolic of Jesus Christ. This is because the Greek word *ichthus*, meaning fish, is spelled with the first letters of the phrase: Jesus Christ, God's Son, Savior. The use of this acronym enabled early Christians to avoid persecution by the Romans, who did not mind how many fish they ate. Saints Andrew and Peter were fishermen before becoming two of the Twelve Apostles. Jesus called them "fishers of men."

In a story reminiscent of Noah, the Hindu god Vishnu assumes the avatar of a fish to warn the sage Manu of a coming flood. A fish, which Manu saves by kindness, returns to advise him to build a boat. He does so, and is able to moor it to Vishnu himself, manifested as a one-horned, golden-scaled gigantic fish.

In Western astrology, people born under the sign of Pisces are believed to be artistic and emotional, in touch with their deeper psyche. This fits with Jungian psychologist Anthony Stevens' view, which identifies water creatures as symbolic of the collective unconscious. The deeper the layers of self-knowledge, the more defined is the personality. Thus, the fish is a symbol of the Self. The surfacing of a fish from water is viewed as the acquisition of personal knowledge.

Yet as the unconscious aspect of our selves is not under our direct control, neither are slippery, flopping fish. The uncontrollable, potent energy of the unconscious can be symbolized by a fish that one hopes to bait to the surface.

Fish are the third most common animal helpers in Cinderella stories. One of the oldest known Cinderella stories is the Chinese *Yeh-Shen*, a magic bones variant in which a fish plays the role of helper. Abused by her stepmother, the girl has no friend in the world other than a fish, which she adopts as a pet. It is killed and eaten by the stepmother, but a mystical Kind Uncle tells Yeh-Shen that the bones contain magic. The same scenario occurs in *Abadeha*, the Phillipine Cinderella, and *The Golden Sandal*, a Cinderella story from Iraq.

This notion of the fish as Self reframes the meaning of some of the Cinderella stories in which the girl begins feeding a portion of her daily rice to her pet fish, at the expense of her own hunger. In the South Pacific Cinderella tale, *The Bones of Djulung*, the girl's pet fish becomes fat while she becomes thin. It seems that diverting energy from the business of daily survival is necessary for personal enlightenment.

Frogs and Toads

Frogs date to the Devonian period of 350 million years ago. The amphibian class *Anura,* which contains both frogs and toads, was the next after fish to evolve from the slime. They are found on each continent save Antarctica, and appear in folklore all over the world.

In African folk tales, frogs seem to have a reputation as wooers of women. Two Angolan stories illustrate this. In *Frog and His Two Wives,* we learn that Frog married two frog-wives and built each a comfortable lodging. One cooked his breakfast and the other his supper, and in this way, both were happy with his company. The first wife he called Kuo-kua, and the second Kua-kuo. One cloudy day neither wife could tell what time it was so they both cooked a meal for him, and called to their husband to come. Frog could not decide how to please them both, and that is why he can be heard croaking even today, calling out, "Kuo-kua! Kua-kuo!"

In a second tale, *Elephant and Frog Go Courting,* the storyteller begins by saying, "Frog and Elephant were enormously popular with the girls," and goes on to enumerate the many ways in which the two animals are alike. Both love water, both love walking through the forest...and both love the ladies. One day while showing off, Frog brags that Elephant is his servant, and carries him on his back whenever he desires a ride through the forest. By trickery, Frog then demonstrates that this is so, riding atop Elephant as they pass the girls' hut. The cocky little amphibian is celebrated as master of the pachyderm. It is interesting to find a parallel for this manly frog in the English folk song, *Froggy Went A-Courtin'*, which has been dated to the year 1580.

In the legends of the Mende people of Sierra Leone, there is a story that the gods sent two messengers down to earth, a toad and a dog. The toad's message was, "Death has come." The dog was supposed to say, "Life has come." But once on earth, the dog, true to its character, got distracted as he passed by some people cooking food. While Dog begged for scraps, Frog continued and delivered his message to the people. If Dog had not failed, death would not be permanent.

A tale from Angola features the son of a great chief, who has been spoiled with everything he has ever wanted. He demands none other than the daughter of the sun and the moon for his wife, and the only messenger who is brave enough to go up to the heavens with the message is a frog. He has shrewdly observed that even the daughter of the sun and the moon fills her water jug each day, sliding down a spider's web to earth. Frog waits for her at the water hole and jumps into her jug while she fills it, and by this means is carried up to heaven.

Because they undergo metamorphosis, changing shape from a legless, swimming tadpole to a tailless, four-legged hopper, frogs are symbols of rebirth and regeneration. The Egyptian goddess Heket, she who protected newborns, was sometimes shown with the face of a frog, and sometimes as an actual frog. Heket is associated with embryonic growth and midwifery and was believed to assist in the birth of the sun each morning.

In American Indian legend, the Great Frog Spirit is a bringer of rain. Frogs are said to have masculine connotations and toads feminine. This connection stems from the fact that toads live in the earth, thereby associating them with Mother Earth. In Japanese mythology, the story of the Great Spirit of the Toad follows this pattern. In that fable, a thief who tries to steal from an old woman is thwarted when she transforms into a powerful man and then vanishes. The voice of the old woman then tells the thief, "You have offended me, the Great Spirit of the Toad, and you must earn your forgiveness." He is cursed with a toad upon his shoulder to remind him of his wicked ways, and sent out to work among the poor and needy. After awhile, the man realizes how much suffering he is alleviating with his work, and comes to see the toad as a blessed helper. The reformed thief, whose name was Jiraiya, was then known as the "Knight of the Toad."

Frogs and toads, as water creatures, symbolize the deeper strata of self-knowledge, just as fish do. Yet they can exit this aquatic medium, jumping over to become land dwellers. This "hopping about on the threshold between consciousness and unconsciousness," as Anthony Stevens notes in *Ariadne's Thread*, makes the frog a powerful force, a representative of hidden desires.

Bruno Bettelheim said that the fairy tale frog serves an important sex education role in many stories involving maidens. The story of *The Frog King* is one example. In this story, a young princess drops her ball into a pond. A frog offers to retrieve it, but only for a price. The princess makes a promise to the frog that he can eat from her plate and sleep by her bed, but then tries to break her word. She is disgusted by the frog when he comes to sleep with her, yet her father insists that she honor her vow to let him into her bed. After some delay, she does so, and the girl then embraces him as "a dear companion and husband" just as her father wished.

Bettelheim believed that the animal's literal transformation from tadpole to frog is a metaphor for a child's physical development into an adult. Thus it shows us that a girl too young for a romantic partner is repelled by the idea of a physical relationship, while after she matures, her feelings change.

Marie Louise von Franz, an associate of Dr. Carl Jung, traces this connection more directly. She identifies a "widespread ritual for a love charm in German, Swiss and Austrian" countries, involving the bones of a frog. A young man in love must feed a live frog to swarming ants. When the creature is reduced to bone, he can take the leg bone, and discreetly touch the woman he admires with it. This is said to induce feelings of love. Similar rituals may be the reason why the ground bodies of frogs and toads are said to be ingredients in witches' potions.

Frogs appear in the Indian Cinderella story of *Bopaluchi*, where they croak a warning to her about a man who falsely claims to be her uncle. In the Korean version, a frog helps Pear Blossom avoid a beating by squeezing itself into the hole in the bottom of a jar she must fill with water.

Frogs are popular characters in contemporary children's books. The *I Can Read: Frog and Toad* Series, by Caldecott and Newbery Awards winner Arnold Lobel pits innocent, impulsive Toad against his more mature and thoughtful friend Frog. Mercer Mayer's all-picture classic, *A Boy, a Dog and a Frog* is another example. Perhaps the most famous American frog of all is Kermit the Frog, beloved of *Sesame Street* fame.

Lizards

All lizards are members of the order *Squamata*, sub-order *Sauria*. They are an ancient creature found on all seven continents. There are thousands of species of lizards, most ranging in size from one inch to one foot in length. Lizards are generally no threat to human beings: the gila monster, *Heloderma suspectum*, and the Mexican beaded lizard are the only two members of *Helodermatidae*, the family of poisonous lizards. All lizards have long tails and conspicuous eyes. Some species have transparent eyelids, allowing them to "see" with their eyes closed.

The members of the Chameleon family, which includes around one hundred species, have some truly unusual features that lend themselves to fantasy. The appearance of the chameleon's protruding eyeballs, which can swivel independently of each other, enhances the effect of hidden power. Their ability to remain motionless, then dart away at lightning speed, lends them an air of serene enlightenment. Chameleon's hormonally driven change of skin color, according to ambient temperature and surroundings, and the jettisoning of their tails for escape from predators can seem like wizardry. As most of us know, there are times in life when a second chance is more valuable than gold.

Ancient cultures of the Pacific Islands believe that lizards are incarnations of a family's forefathers, or that they are messengers from the gods. They are felt to be beneficent creatures, worthy of respect. It is interesting to see the opposite feeling in most European folklore. Here lizards are associated with the occult and used as ingredients in witch's spells.

Lizards appear in African mythology as messengers from heaven and precursors to mankind. Two chameleons play starring roles in a Zulu creation myth. They say that Unkulunkulo, The Very Old, sent a chameleon out to tell his newly created people that they would never die. But this lizard stopped to warm himself along the way, and by the time he got to the village, The Very Old one had changed his mind, and sent a second chameleon to tell the villagers that they would, indeed, die.

In the legend of the Pahouin tribe in South Africa, "God created man with clay, first in the shape of a lizard, which he put in a pond and left there for seven days, after which he ordered him out. A man came out of the pond instead of a lizard."

Lizard legends were brought to the United States by African slaves. In one Br'er Rabbit story, that crafty rabbit is bested, for once, by Br'er Lizard, who uses a magical sword to harvest crops.

Because lizards are an ancient line of animals, Jungian psychologists believe the lizard to be representative of an element of the Self that is deeply buried in the unconscious.

The introduction of lizards as helpers to Cinderella seems to have come from the seventeenth-century author Charles Perrault. In his version, six lizards were transformed into coachmen by a fairy godmother, perhaps because of the animal's European ties to witchcraft.

Sea Serpents and Dragons

Close cousins to the lizard are the dragon and the serpent, especially the sea serpent. The earliest dragons are depicted as water creatures in both Western and Eastern mythology. They are celebrated in the Asian tradition as the male aspect of the universe, or *yang* principle, to be revered, celebrated, and feared. They are one of the stars of the Lunar New Year celebration, held to bring good luck. The four dragon kings of Chinese mythology are said to rule over the four seas and to live in the sky. They control both drought and flood. As creatures of the air they were believed to be divine due to their proximity with the gods.

Sea serpents are gigantic, man-eating monsters
and often bedevil sailors. One of the most famous
of these beasts in Western mythology is Grendel,
the brute slain by Beowulf. This Danish legend of
pre-Christianity tells of the hero Beowulf and his
mighty single-handed defeat of the behemoth
underwater creature.

In Greek mythology, Perseus, son of Zeus
(Jupiter) and Danae, slays a sea serpent in order to
free the lovely Andromeda, who has been chained
to a rock as a gift to appease it. The monster had
been sent by the vengeful Sea Nymphs to punish
Andromeda's mother for her self-conceit and vani-
ty.

In Japanese myth, it is the unpredictable god
Susanoo, child of the sun and moon, who slays a
serpent. He was believed to have two souls, Ara-
mi-tama, the wicked one, and Nigi-mi-tama, the
peaceful one. As a hero on earth, he saved the
eighth and last daughter of a couple menaced by a
maiden-eating snake. His plan involved first changing the girl into a comb that he tucked into his hair,
before luring the monster with the scent of bowls of
rice wine. Snakes, thunder, and water are connected
to Susanoo.

The ancient Chinese believed dragons to be rain-
makers, causing thunder and lighting by their fight-
ing amongst themselves.

One story about a Japanese dragon relates the
story of a young man by the name of Anchin. This
young traveller flirted with the daughter of an
innkeeper. Promising that he would marry her on

his return trip, he journeyed on. The girl waited and waited, and soon found out through other travelers that Anchin was home already. The jilted girl became an angry dragon, tracked him down, and sizzled his flesh.

Reports of Western dragons date to pre-Roman times. In approximatly 430 C.E., King Vortigern of the Angle tribe faced an invasion by Saxon brothers Hengist and Horsa. These warriors arrived with three longships of soldiers, having travelled down from northern Europe. Vortigern tried to avoid battling them by offering them land and friendship, and engaging them to help him battle the Picts. That tribe was notorious both for their tinted and tattooed skin and for their warlike ways.

Vortigern, who eventually married Horsa's daughter, was betrayed by his own son, Vortimer. Astrologers thought it prudent for Vortigern to construct a fortress in Welsh territory. Yet when supplies of "timber and stones were brought, they kept sinking into the earth and the builders could make no gains." Again the astrologers were consulted, and this time they recommended stronger measures. A male child with no father must be found and sacrificed on the foundation stones. Such a boy was soon found —but what he told the King was troubling. Beneath the chosen site, said the boy, lay an underground lake, in which two dragons lived, one red and one white. The pit was opened, and the dragons released. The beasts battled and the boy, watching first the white dragon gain, and then the red, interpreted the meaning of the action for the king. The white dragon represented the Saxons, the red one the Britons. The Britons would eventually prevail over the Saxons, said the boy—but King Vortigern would not live to see this.

In England today you can still see the White Horse of Uffington, a three hundred seventy-four foot long image carved into the chalk hillside of the land. Below this massive pictogram is a hill known as Dragon Hill. Legend says that it is there that St. George, the original knight in shining armor, did battle. Sometime before the year 700 C.E. a warrior slew a dragon that had been eating one maiden a day from the neighboring kingdom. As it happened, this man passed by on the very day that the King's daughter, dressed in bridal white and chained to a rock, was on the menu. George offered to kill the dragon in exchange for the conversion of the populace to Christianity. Both sides kept their bargain, and the maiden was set free.

The image of St. George's red cross against a white background is the symbol of England. It is superimposed on the blue and white cross of Scotland for the flag of the United Kingdom.

St. Michael, one of the four archangels, slew Satan in the form of a dragon. The fight is described in Revelation, when "God's temple in heaven opened," and a pregnant woman, in a dress of the sun, with the moon on her feet, appeared. Immediately after this apparition came "an enormous red dragon with seven heads and ten horns" which Michael defeated by tossing the beast to the ground, along with its evil angels. St. Michael is the patron saint of warriors.

Western dragons, like those of the East, are associated with water. The Roman historian Herodotus filed reports of a "flying serpent" that attacked Egypt and was killed by the ibises along the River Nile. Vikings carved dragons on the prows of their warships, as fetishes of power and invocations of war. In Ireland, sometime around the 4th century C.E., Saint Patrick drove the snakes off of the island, but couldn't manage the dragons. Their primordial magic proved too powerful for him. The best he could do was to condemn them to the seas.

European dragons are sometimes winged and sometimes not. The classical description of the beast came about during the medieval period, which covered roughly the 2nd through 4th centuries. Specifically, this is the head of a fire-breathing lion, the body of a scaled reptile, and the personality of an avaricious miser and mercenary. As Christianity spread, dragons were said to be incarnations of Satan. Thus, dragon-slayers such as Arthur, the "semi-mystical chieftain of the 6th century" (Bulfinch, 1855) and his descendants, including St. George of the 13th century, were symbolically killing the Dark One himself.

Dragons in children's literature are not always brave. Ogden Nash's *The Tale of Custard the Dragon* (1936), features a little girl named Belinda, who "lives in a little white house, with a little black kitten and a little gray mouse." She also has a little black dog who is "sharp as mustard" and a cowardly dragon, "and she called him Custard."

The Reluctant Dragon (1938) dreamed up by author Kenneth Grahame of *Wind in the Willows* fame, was a poetic type, saved by a boy who befriends him. The weeping *Puff The Magic Dragon* of his namesake song (Lipton & Yarrow, 1963) was inspired by Custard. The song became a hit for the band Peter, Paul and Mary.

American dragons made their debut in the 1887 tall tale, *The Bee-Man of Orn*, who saves a town from being menaced by a dragon with the help of his beehives. That tale is not well known, but a later one by the same author, Frank Stockton, is a short story classic, *The Lady and the Tiger*. (N. Philip, *American Fairy Tales,* 1996). Later American dragons were kinder and gentler. In 1948, Ruth Stiles Gannet began the *My Father's Dragon* series. A nine-year-old boy comes to the aid of a baby dragon, "about the size of a large, black bear, [with] a long tail and yellow and blue stripes. His horn and the bottoms of his feet are bright red, and he has gold-colored wings."

Graeme Base, writing under the *nomme du plume* Rowland W. Greasebeam, B.Sc., combines natural history with fantasy in his detailed picture dictionary, *The Discovery of Dragons: New Research Revealed*. He lists the Two-Headed Peruvian Mountain Draak and the Western Skull-Faced Rattleworm as American dragon species. (1996)

English author C. S. Lewis invented a more traditional dragon for *The Voyage of the Dawn Treader* (1952). When quarrelsome Eustace Clarence Scrubb hides to avoid his share of hard work when the ship lands, he encounters a dying dragon's lair. Eustace hides, then falls asleep among the gems. When he awakens, he has been transformed into a dragon.

The 1992 publication of James Gurney's *Dinotopia* illustrates the connection between dinosaurs and dragons. His beasts are intelligent and have the gift of speech. They are intellectuals with well-developed cultural traditions and skilled craftsmen. His story tells of a father and son shipwrecked on their island.

A dragon story that bridges the gap between Eastern and Western is *Everyone Knows What a Dragon Looks Like* (Jay Williams and Mercer Mayer, 1984). Mercer Meyer's gorgeous illustrations make this picture book come alive. Here a poor street sweeper is able to save his village because he alone believes a disguised dragon that comes to warn the people of the invading Huns. This parable offers marvelous depictions of the Chinese scenery and a tongue-in-cheek title that piques interest in the diversity of dragon lore.

Mice

Rodentia myomorpha is a classification that covers both mice and rats, along with about one thousand other species of small gnawing mammals. Its members are divided into nine families that include voles, hamsters and lemmings. The *Muridae* family and its many branches includes bamboo rats and jumping mice. However, it is the mouse tribe *Mus musculus* that identifies the house mouse and its multitudes of generations. These little animals originated in Southeast Asia and have spread all over the world. Wherever people are found, mice are there to nibble on as much of our food as they can get at.

Mice were used as ingredients in household remedies for earache in ancient Greece and bedwetting in 18th century New England. They are believed to be the familiars of witches in many cultures and are staples used in cursing, spell-binding and potion-making the world over. In Bohemia it was believed that sighting a white mouse brought good luck. In China and other parts of Asia, the mouse is considered to be the "separable soul" of a sleeping person, thus enhancing their association with the occult.

In German folklore mice are said to have been made by witches out of scraps of leather and cloth, while in Christian mythology they were made by the Devil himself, sent to pester Noah and his ark full of animals.

Jungian psychologists believe that mice are symbols of the unconscious processes of thought and problem solving: as nagging thoughts nibble around the edge of our consciousness, so do mice nibble around the barriers between them and food.

Mice often appear as helpers in stories, perhaps because they are a ubiquitous animal, familiar to people everywhere. The power of one mouse is demonstrated in the 4th century C.E. Aesop's Fable, *The Lion and the Mouse.* In this story, thought to have originated in Asia, a lion catches a mouse audacious enough to run over his face while he is sleeping. The mouse begs mercy and promises that if the lion frees him, he will help the lion one day in return. The King of the Jungle laughs, and, for the sake of a good joke, agrees. The very next day the lion is snared by a hunter. Hearing his roars of anguish, the mouse comes to the lion's aid, gnawing through the strap holding its paw. The big cat now understands the maxim, "No one is too small to be able to help a friend."

The story of the "town mouse" and the "country mouse" is found in countries on several continents including Africa, Europe and North America. In this narrative, a house mouse used to foraging in the wild encounters a friendly city mouse. This arrogant creature informs her that the poor food eaten by country mice is nothing compared to the rich meals city mice eat. So the country mouse goes to visit the city. She is shocked by the danger of stealing cheeses and other human food from under the noses of cats, drawing the moral *No luxury is worth the price of living in constant fear.*

Mice are among the most common helpers in Cinderella stories. In the Russian cluster of folk-tales featuring the witch Baba Yaga, who eats children with her iron teeth, many animals act as helpers, including cows, birds, and mice. In the story of *Baba Yaga and the Kind Hearted Girl*, a cruel stepmother forces a child to go and beg for a needle and thread from the witch in the forest. A little mouse, with whom the girl has shared her crumbs, gives her detailed guidance on how to get the needle and escape with her life. After it all ends, and the girl and her tiny friend are safe and sound, the last scene is "mousey-kins" warming its tiny paws on the girl's hot glass of tea.

Mice are included in the 1697 retelling of *Cinderilla, or The Little Glass Slipper*, by Frenchman Charles Perrault. The "godmother, who was really a fairy," transformed six living mice into horses to draw Cinderella's carriage. His choice of them may be due to then-common associations of mice with witches and magic. It may also have sprung from his imagination that mice and horses have similarities. Both are four-legged mammals with tails, both have pointed heads, and both were common household animals. Their main difference, to the naked eye, is size. Mice appear in all Perrault-based Cinderella stories as horses, and in many other variants as peripheral characters. There is a Cinderella story from Finland involving a request for a mouse skin cloak.

Mice of literature include many scurrying through Mother Goose rhymes. There are the Three Blind Mice and the Mouse that "ran up the clock." These rhymes date to the fifteenth century and were included in Perrault's first book of children's stories.

One of the most famous folk songs of England, later brought to the United States, describes *The Frog Who Would A-Wooing Go or A Moste*

Strange Weddinge of the Frogge and the Mouse, as it was published in 1580. It is still a popular tune, better known today as "Froggie Went A-Courting." The object of his courtship is the lovely Miss Mouse.

The title character of Beatrix Potter's 1910 children's story, *The Tale of Mrs. Tittlemouse*, is a homey little wood mouse. She bustles around her nest like an English granny, chasing beetles off her clean swept floors and fetching "cherry-stones and thistle-down seeds" from a storeroom. Potter included many mouse characters as foils for the cats and rabbits in her other books.

The 1945 American classic, *Stuart Little*, concerns the adventures of Stuart, a mouse-child born to Mr. and Mrs. Frederick C. Little. They adore their son—despite the fact that he is only a two-inch-high rodent. The book was written by E. B. White of *Charlotte's Web* fame. His inspiration may have come from the many fairy tales where a childless couple adopts an animal or tiny being. Jacob and Wilhelm Grimm's first collection of tales included the story of *Hans, My Hedgehog*, born in similar circumstances.

In 1952, C.S. Lewis wrote *The Voyage of the Dawn Treader*, Book Three in the Chronicles of Narnia. Reepicheep, a vain and valiant mouse and loyal servant to King Caspian, fights all comers including sea monsters to defend the world of Aslan, the lion deity of Narnia.

Another brave fictional mouse is *Runaway Ralph*. Written by Beverly Cleary in 1971, the book follows "a small brown mouse named Ralph" that has been given a mouse-sized motorcycle by a little boy. He rides away on it, of course, bound for glory and adventure.

The last decade of the twentieth century witnessed the emergence of the altruistic mouse society of *Redwall*, from the imagination of Brian Jacques. In this twelve book epic, Luke the mouse warrior, and later, his son Martin, join together with moles, badgers and birds to fight against the sea-faring pirate rats and their gang of vicious stoats and weasels. This medieval themed saga of the mice's history, from the first defense of their woodlands to the founding of Redwall Abbey, features a society of tiny mouse-monks, who wear sandals and coarse-cloth habits. They feast on nut bread and ale.

Rabbits and Hares

These furry mammals comprise the two families of the order *Lagomorpha*. There are more than fifty species of rabbits and hares and they are found on the continents of Africa, Asia, Europe, and the Americas. Rabbits are mighty procreators, making them ancient symbols of fertility and springtime. Everywhere that rabbits and hares live, they appear as characters in folk and fairy tales. Often, but not always, they are tricksters.

In Burma, India and Tibet, rabbits star as clever figures, able to outwit larger, fiercer animals, at least most of the time. In Vietnam, they say that a clever rabbit once survived a drought by eating sweet potatoes in the farmer's vegetable patch.

When the farmer saw him, the rabbit played dead. But he tried the trick once too many times, and was finally caught by the farmer and put into a basket for dinner. Back in the farmer's hut, the rabbit peeked out from the basket he was stuck under, and noticed a big fish in a basin. He tricked the fish into jumping out of the basin just as the farmer came in. When the farmer grabbed the basket to catch the fish, the rabbit hopped away.

The South African character of Hare finds himself tricked by cunning Miss Tortoise in an old tale. After convincing Tortoise to help him raid a field of yams, and then trying to keep the tubers all for himself, he finds that Tortoise has instead fooled him, and eaten the lot. Tortoise tricks Hare again, of course, in the Aesop's Fable describing the famous race between the two of them. This ends with cocky Hare outwitted and the familiar moral: *Slow and steady wins the race.* In other African tales, Rabbit outwits the lion, the hyena, and the crocodile.

American black folk tales, including the Tar Baby and Bre'r Rabbit, are direct transplants from Africa, where they were called Gum Baby or Hare. Bre'r Rabbit is renowned as wily, brave, and forever getting the better of his so-called superiors.

In one such story, Bre'r Rabbit and Bear are sent by the other animals to ask Lion to stop roaring so loudly all the time.

From a safe distance, Bre'r Rabbit calls out, "Hear tell you are scarin' everybody, all the little animals, with your roarin' all the time."

Lion bellows, "ME AND MYSELF AND ME AND MYSELF AND ME AND MYSELF! And no one tells me what to do!"

But Bre'r Rabbit tricks him into an introduction to Man, after which Lion is appropriately respectful, and turns his volume down.

In others, the rascally rabbit gets the greens, or the goods, or whatever there is to be gotten, standing in for the underdog everywhere. Another American rabbit that always seems to get his way is Bugs Bunny, who famously posed the question, "What's up, Doc?"

American Indians used rabbits and hares as food and sources of fur, but respected them as intelligent, resourceful animals. Rabbits are favorite tricksters in tribes from the Great Lakes Area, including the Potawatomi, who lived on the banks of Lake Michigan.

In China, they say that two sisters once lived in the moon. They worked their silk embroidery by its light, but when they realized that all of the people on earth were watching them, they moved to the sun. Now only the Jade Moon Rabbit lives there, along with Cheng-O, the Moon Lady. She is doomed to spend most of the year there away from her husband, after stealing his Pill of Eternal Life. Each October, during the Moon Festival, she is believed to come back to earth.

In Japan, they tell of the Rabbit in the Moon. Long ago, a rabbit lived in a small hut with his companions, the fox and the monkey. One night a stranger came seeking shelter, and they let him in.

The fox went out and caught a fish for the guest, and the monkey picked some fruit. The rabbit could not very well offer the visitor grass, yet he had nothing else. In a moment of selfless generosity, the little rabbit jumped into the flames of the hearth fire, knowing that roast rabbit would make the gentleman a fine meal. The fellow, who was the chief of the gods, disguised so that he could test those he met, was impressed. He gathered the bunny's bones and arranged them on the moon in his image. It is still visible today. In the Western world it may be the Man in the Moon people look for, but not everywhere.

In one of the Jataka tales of Buddha, *The Foolish, Timid Rabbit*, the animal is cast in the role of Henny-Penny, who feels a drop of rain on her head and sounds the alarm that the sky is falling. In the Buddha story a coconut falls from a tree, causing Rabbit to tear through the forest in panic. He is followed by the fox, the deer and the elephant. It is Lion who calms the animals and locates the object that startled Rabbit.

The rabbit's talent for avoiding harm makes it a good luck charm. The concept of *sympathetic magic*, in which the powers of the whole extend to any small piece, leads to the practice of using rabbit's skin and rabbit's foot amulets in the United States and other countries.

One American Cinderella story, *The Talking Eggs*, (Robert D. San Souci, 1989) is based on an African-American folktale. It features a Baba Yaga or witch-woman who encounters a young girl by the well. The girl is courteous to her, so the old woman invites her back to her cottage. Here the girl carefully follows the instructions the witch gives her, and is rewarded with a show of square dancing rabbits dressed in finery, as well as the gift of eggs which contain jewels and gold. These themes reflect those in *Chinye: a West African Folktale*, retold by Obi Onyefulu (1994).

An Italian variant of the *Catskin Cinderella*, in which the girl's father insists that she become his wife, features an escape by means of rabbits. The girl delays him by asking for three dresses, one after another, and each finer than the last. Instead of delaying the marriage as she had hoped, her father easily gets each dress. Finally she asks for a cloak made of rabbit skins. When she has procured this, she flees. It is by means of the cloak that she hides herself from her father and transforms into an exotic princess, thus marrying the prince.

Rabbits of literature include the infamous Peter Rabbit, who "lived under the banks of a very big fir tree" and imprudently nibbled the cucumbers in Mr. McGregor's garden. Lewis Carroll's *Alice's Adventures in Wonderland* featured the White Rabbit who leads Alice down the hole, and the March Hare who presides over a wacky tea party.

Twenty-first century vestiges of rabbits' role as symbols of spring and renewal are still found in the American Easter Bunny, also known as Peter Cottontail. In Europe, rabbits are traditional elements of Easter as well. Candies and cakes are made in their shape in many countries.

Rats

Rattus rattus, the black rat, is native to Southeast Asia. Claiming over one hundred species, the rat family is now found worldwide. They are clever survivors who can live easy lives off the refuse of humans. Rat society is complex and hierarchical.

Rats have been considered pests as long as they have lived among humans. They are considered to be associates of the Devil in European folklore. Their association with death dates at least back to the Black Plague of Europe during the thirteenth century, that killed one in three people in affected areas. Rats brought sorrow to the German town of Hamelin in the year 1284, when one hundred thirty children were kidnapped by a piper. The town was swarming with rats, so many that, according to Robert Browning's 1888 poem commemorating the event:

They fought the dogs and killed the cats,
  and bit the babies in the cradles,
    and ate the cheeses out of the vats,
  and licked the soup from cook's own ladles.

When the rat-catcher could not stop this horror, the townspeople turned to a stranger who had come into town. He offered to lead the vermin away by playing a tune on his pipe. His price was one thousand gilders, which the Mayor eagerly agreed to. Until the job was done, that is—then the greedy politicians would not pay the price. So the piper played another tune, and every child in town followed him. The people pursued the parade of children until it reached the foot of a mountain:

When, lo, as they reached the mountain-side,
a wondrous portal opened wide,
as if a cavern was suddenly hollowed;
and the Piper advanced and the children followed,
and when all were gone to the very last,
the door in the mountain-side shut fast.

The town of Hamelin is still a busy town, and the *Rattenflängerhaus*, the official residence of the rat-catcher, still exists.

A classical Chinese poem is cited by Jungian psychologist Marie Louise von Franz as reflecting the underlying symbolism of rats as archetypes. It reads:

Rat in my brain,
I cannot sleep, day and night
You gnaw out of me my life.
I am slowly falling away,
Oh, rat in my brain,
Oh, my bad conscience.
Will you never give me peace again!

The rat, with its unceasing chewing, can represent thoughts that keep us awake at night. Thus, rats are also *psychopomps*, animal characters that lead us, tantalizingly, into the crevices of our psyche. Snakes and moles carry similar meaning.

It is a rat that ate the malt that triggered the age-old English nursery rhyme, *The House That Jack Built*. That rat was promptly killed by a cat that was "chased by a dog which is tossed by a cow (with a crumpled horn) that is milked by a maiden (all forlorn), who is kissed by a man (all tattered and torn) and married by the priest, (all shaven and shorn)."

In the Japanese zodiac, People of the Rat are seen as humble and as being successful through perseverance. Maybe something of these qualities is the reason that rats are traditionally cast in Cinderella stories as the coachman, courtesy of the fairy godmother. This character was described by Perrault as "huge" and bearded. The godmother, "who was a Fairy," "touched him with her wand [and] he was turned into a fat, jolly coach-man, that had the finest whiskers ever seen."

The rats of Beatrix Potter's *The Roly-Poly Pudding or The Tale of Samuel Whiskers* were not so jolly. A rat couple trap fat little Tom Kitten, who has gone exploring in the woodwork, and leave him while they forage for ingredients:

> Presently the rats came back and set to work to make him into a dumpling. First they smeared him with butter, and then they rolled him in the dough. "Will not the string be very indigestible, Anna Maria?" inquired Samuel Whiskers. Anna Maria said that she thought that it was of no consequence; but she wished that Tom Kitten would hold his head still, as it disarranged the pastry. She laid hold of his ears.

Potter dedicated this little book "In remembrance of 'SAMMY,' the intelligent, pink-eyed representative of a persecuted (but irrepressible) race, an affectionate little friend, and most accomplished thief."

Rats of contemporary literature include those from Robert O'Brien's *Mrs. Frisby and the Rats of NIMH,* (1971) in which super-rats genetically engineered by humans escape their lab and aid woodland creatures.

In Brian Jacques's *Redwall* series, rats are evil creatures, representative of boot-jack soldiers and brutal repression. One such character is Nadaz, "the purple-robed leader" of a coven of black-robed rats who scheme from an underground cavern.

In the 1999 Garth Nix fantasy story *Blackbeard the Pirate,* Leonardo Rattinci, with his "special sorcerous orreries," and pirate rats wearing "old fashioned clothes with big wide belts and floppy hats," carry cutlasses in their paws. Here a boy follows the rats down a sewer pipe, and ends up doing battle with the fearsome Blackbeard.

Part Three

Rings and Things:
The Symbolism of Objects

Ashes and Cinders

Learning to control fire moved humanity one major step up the survival chain, and several steps farther from the animal mentality. Spear points carbonized by fire led to sharper spears, and therefore more successful hunts. More meat and the ability to cook it meant better nutrition. Less time spent hunting created more free time for reflection, and, since a campfire repelled wild animals, it was then safer for social interactions after dark. The ability to keep evil spirits away probably seemed a logical extension of fire's power.

Sacred fires go back as far as human history. The Celtic observance of Samhain, on October 31st, was seen as the last night of summer, and a time when the power of light waned. The Druid priests who presided over the ceremonies ordered all household fires to be extinguished on that night. The belief that restless spirits were afoot encouraged all members of the community to gather for a bonfire, and coals from it were then carried home to rekindle each hearth.

The concept of sympathetic magic, in which an event or item gains power because it is part of something else which is perceived to be powerful, is widespread among world culture. For the early people of the British Isles, if the fire itself was sacred, so were the coals taken from it. Even the ashes, considered "relics of the fire," were seen as potent, and carried as charms or mixed into the soil as crops were planted.

Ashes were used in religious rites by Aztec priests, who rubbed them on their faces prior to prayers. This is strikingly similar to the Catholic tradition of marking a cross on the face with ashes to signify mourning for Jesus, as is done on Ash Wednesday. The ceremony marks the beginning of Lent, which is the interval between Jesus' crucifixion and his resurrection on Easter Sunday. Because Jesus is said to have died for humanity's sins, those marked with ashes meditate on repentance and humility.

For thousands of years, fire was the means by which people kept warm and cooked food. The hearth was literally the heart of the home in the times when one lived or died by what was in the family cooking pot or woodpile. Early people understood this, and their fire deities were beings of great importance. The Roman goddess Vesta, called Hestia by the Greeks, was a European goddess of the hearth. She presided over the daily matters of each family, not unlike the Kitchen God's Wife of

Chinese mythology, described in Amy Tan's 1993 novel. Vesta's temple was tended by six young virgins who kept her sacred fire burning day and night. It is from her that we draw the expression "to keep the home fires burning," meaning that someone is at home, attending to family matters.

The everyday reality of building a fire to cook each meal, then cleaning the hearth, then gathering fuel to cook the next meal, meant hard work and dirty clothes. That is why the lowest ranking servant, often a child, was assigned this task. A fire built from wood leaves behind several kinds of residue. If weather and wood are dry, complete combustion occurs, and leaves little behind. *Ashes* are the gray or white, powdered specks which can be scattered with a breath, or marked with the faintest pressure. As abundant as they were in any household, ashes became key ingredients in many home cures and traditions. In North Africa, they are mixed with water to make a soothing eye wash. In England they were scattered around a baby's cradle to detect night visitors, whether animal or spirit.

Cinders are the larger particles, the bits of wood that have not completely burned. They may also be live, in the state of being almost—but not quite—ignited. Cinders can appear ashy and gray on the outside, but are easily kindled into flames. The cold leftovers which need to be cleaned from the hearth before a new fire can be laid are also called soot. *Soot* is the black, powdery flakes of carbonized wood from an incompletely burned fire. Any one who handles a lot of them is quite soon filthy, and their clothes are stained with grime.

Bruno Bettelheim, the educator and psychologist who analyzed *Cinderella* and other fairy tales in his 1977 *The Uses of Enchantment: the Meaning and Importance of Fairy Tales*, calls *Cinderella* "the best known fairy tale." He cites the historic connotations of the expression "living among the cinders" in Germany and other parts of Europe. There, the phrase meant to be the outcast of the family, the least prosperous sibling.

The world-wide body of Cinderella-type tales describing dirty, ill-treated drudges who suddenly make good, usually features a female child. The names of the stories are generally based on various combinations of the words ashes, cinders, and soot. In the United States, a regional variant is Ashpet, in England she is Ash Wench or Ash Maiden.

The German word for ashes is *asche*; and names for this character in the region where the Brothers Grimm collected stories include *Aschenputtel, Aschenpüster,* and *Aschenbrödel.* These are all quaint ways of describing small household items which sit by the hearth: buckets and pots and other necessary but unlovely things.

In French, both ashes and cinders are defined as *cendre*, and the character is called *Cendrillon*. This is a gender-neutral term and literally means "one who lives among cinders. The feminine form is *Cinderilla* or *Cinderella*, which has been translated into English as *Cinderbreeches, Cinderbutt, Cinderslut,* and *Cinderwench*.

In Spanish, the girl is generally called *Cenicienta*, and in Italian she is *La Cenerentola*. The Ojibwe American Indian tale of *Sootface Girl*, and the Russian *Mashka Soplivka*, or *Mary the Smutty-Nosed*, are less common derivatives from the word *soot*.

As the woman of the house, Cinderella's mother would certainly have presided over the hearth before she died. Household fireplaces were often quite large and built with a flat top for sleeping on, or a wide hearth for sitting on. Warmth as well as nostalgia may explain why the girl sought comfort there, but there are more complex interpretations. Bettelheim, using Freudian analysis, based his hypothesis on a distinction between ashes, which are clean residue, and cinders, which are dirty. He said that the girl's life among the ashes demonstrated mourning and moral purity.

According to Marie Loiuse von Franz, who was a colleague of Dr. Carl Jung, ashes are simply evidence of fire, which is representative of passion and transformation. Cinders, which von Franz defines as "the still-glowing embers of a blaze," contain the power of metamorphosis. The red-hot centers are hidden by a dusty covering, ready to burst into flame when circumstances permit. So too is Cinderella's beauty and worth concealed by her soot and rags, and so too does it burst forth.

Because the hearth carries such a significant and genuine connection to survival and comfort, it is an archetypal image evoking home and basic security. The fireplace as a symbol of happiness and prosperity continues to be a strong one in the twenty-first century. This is so even as most children in America do not have fireplaces in their homes, and most of their parents did not grow up cooking over open flames.

The ancient people who drove away the evil spirits of Samhain with a crackling blaze were not so different than we are. They used fire to cook with, of course, but they also used it for entertainment. Today's marshmallow roasts and beach fires can be seen as evidence of the nostalgia felt by our collective unconscious. Telling ghost stories around a campfire feels right to us because it is part of our ancient social heritage. We seem to know, on some deep level, that there are still goblins in the dark. The psychological power of "man's red flower" still blazes brightly.

Pumpkins, calabashes and gourds

In Africa, Asia, the Pacific Islands, and parts of North America, two families of these plants grow wild. *Cucurbiticeae lagenaria siceria* is a vine group that includes pumpkins, calabashes, and watermelons. *Bignoniaceae crescentia cujete* are gourd varieties that grow on trees. Both produce large fruits that can easily be hollowed out and used as containers, and many varieties have edible flesh.

These related vegetables appear often in legends and folklore in the countries where they are native. In the United States, the pumpkin is the very essence of two important holidays, Halloween and Thanksgiving. In African and West Indian folklore, witches who use calabashes as magic mirrors are frequent characters. The biggest shells were cut in half and filled to the brim with water, and the images reflected on the surface were believed to foretell the future.

A creation myth from the Hawaiian Islands tells of the three gods who existed "in the time of deep darkness, before the memory of man." They were Kane, the god of creation; Ku, the god of the forests, and Kanaloa, god of the "vast, endless sea." The world began when Kane saw a gigantic calabash floating on the waves. He picked it up and threw it up in the air. The calabash broke apart: the top half of the sphere became the sky. Two big pieces became the sun and the moon. Its seeds scattered across the heavens, becoming stars.

The story of *Two Brothers and Their Magic Gourds*, from Korea, follows a familiar fairy tale theme. On his deathbed, a wealthy man leaves his estate to be equally divided by his two sons. The elder, Nolbu, is mean and miserly, the younger son, Hungbu, is kind and gentle. Soon Hungbu's wife is waiting on Nolbu's like a servant, and his children are going hungry. When Hungbu's little ones cry for more rice, Nolbu's wife "swats them on their cheeks with her large rice paddle, leaving hot grains stuck to their faces."

Now Hungbu takes his family away. They work together to build a hut, and swallows come to nest under the eaves. One day, when the eggs have hatched and the chicks are still nest-bound, a snake comes. It kills all of the swallows, save one, which is knocked to the ground. Hungbu gently binds its broken leg, and it recovers. When it returns home for the annual council held by the Swallow Queen, it tells of Hungbu's kindness, and she sends a large, white seed to the good man. It grows quickly, producing five huge gourds. Hungbu's wife harvests them and they yield gold, rice, silk cloth, servants, and a fine home.

Soon, Nolbu hears of his brother's good fortune. He deliberately injures a swallow, crudely binds it leg, and tells it to get him a magic seed. This time the seed that the Swallow Queen sends also yields five gourds. From them come what Nolbu and his wife have earned: wasps, vipers, frogs, and finally a flood. This washes away everything that Nolbu owns. Reduced to begging, he knocks at his brother's door. Kindhearted Hungbu forgives him, and the brothers and their families live happily ever after.

This story could easily be described as a Cinderella tale in which it is the entire household of the youngest sibling that is being abused. The motif of cutting open fruits or eggs to find jewels or vermin appears in European and American stories as well. In China, gourds and calabashes represent wealth and fertility, as do other large, round fruits such as the orange and the pomelo.

Pumpkins and gourds have an ancient connection with spiritualism. The tradition of Halloween, or All Hallows Evening, is actually a combination of the Celtic observance of Samhain and the modern overlay of Christianity. Candle-lit lanterns carved from vegetables have been used for several thousand years in the British Isles. The Druids, who were the religious power of these post-Neolithic people, worshipped many deities of nature with a complex series of rituals. They believed that departed souls returned to earth for one night of the year, the final night of summer. To honor the changing of the season, and to lend strength to the sun as Samhain, Lord Winter, seemed to overpower it, all-night bonfires were held. The people disguised themselves as animals so that evil spirits abroad that night could not recognize them to do malice. Hearth fires in each home were snuffed, and the old ashes swept away. At dawn, each family carried home "new fire" for the first day of the new year, in a lantern or hollowed-out potato. These coals were used to kindle a fresh hearth fire, and believed to keep the family safe until the following Samhain.

It was during the 17th century that St. Boniface of England had the idea of moving the Christian day for honoring the lesser-known saints to the autumn festival time. This attempt to superimpose Christianity over the tradition of night mischief has never been fully successful. In fact, one pagan custom has survived intact.

The American tradition of hollowing out and carving pumpkins on Halloween night, and then lighting them with candles to drive the spirits away still thrives. It was brought to the United States in the 1800's with the mass immigration of Irish, Welsh, and English folks. The Puritans, who had forbidden any celebration of the ancient festivals, were finally outnumbered. The new Americans must have been delighted when they got a look at pumpkins. If you have ever tried to make a jack o' lantern out of a rutabaga you will know why.

One European custom, apparently unique to Paris, France, was to parade a big pumpkin through the streets, decorated in a paper crown and given the face of a king. An Italian gourd-head was painted by the artist Giuseppe Arcimboldo sometime in the 1530's. His series of oil on canvas paintings, *The Four Seasons*, was composed entirely of images of fruits, flowers and vegetation. It includes *L'Automne*, pictured as a funny-faced gentleman. Barrel staves form a shirt-collar and parsnips, potatoes, and wheat stalks create the visage of a man. His bald head is that of a white pumpkin, stem and leaves attached.

Oranges and citrons sometimes substitute for pumpkins. An early collection of folktales was that of Giambattista Basile. He published *Il Pentamerone*, a story cycle similar in format to the *Thousand and One Arabian Nights*, in 1637. A prince with an enchanted wife is required to amuse her with five days of non-stop story-telling. He engages ten of the ugliest women he can find for the task, including "long-nosed Tolla, hunchbacked Popa and flabbergasting Antonella." Each tells one story a day, providing a total of fifty "diversions." The ninth diversion of the fifth day is *The Three Citrons*, an elaborate tale involving a tree that "springs forth and grows in four pinches time" to produce fruit. When they are cut, a fairy springs from each, demanding water.

A variation of this tale comes from the island of Corsica, just off the coast of France. In a story called *The Three Oranges*, an abused girl picks three of these round, juicy fruits. She is quite surprised when a fairy is released from each as she cuts it open. The fairies reward her with her own palace, servants, and riches. A prince she then meets falls in love with her, and they marry.

Pumpkins appear in many Cinderella stories. The nineteenth-century Italian *La Zuccaccia*, or *Little Ugly Gourd*, describes a girl given a dress made from a pumpkin shell. In that tale, the cook hides her from an unwanted marriage by carving a pumpkin shell gown. She finishes by winding a ribbon around the stem and topping it off with a spray of flowers. Fastening this damp hat onto the girl's head she tells her, "Run away, my little pumpkin! Seek your fortune in the world." The girl does so and ends up marrying a prince from a neighboring province. In another Italian tale, *Zuchettina*, a woman actually adopts a little gourd as her child and raises her.

A Yiddish tale from Eastern Europe, the *Princess of the Third Pumpkin*, describes how a prince harvests three pumpkins from the royal garden. As he cuts each one open, a naked princess jumps out, cries for thirst, and runs away. By the time he cuts the third one, he is ready with a dress and a bottle of water, and so is able to catch himself a wife.

Rings and Circles

Rings and circles create both an outer and an inner space, emphasizing that which is contained and that which is excluded. Anklets, bracelets, belts and collars are all considered to be rings, since they encircle a part of the body. The crowns of kings and queens and the halos of angels are circles cloistering the head, signifying divine power. Bracelets and necklaces can symbolize a loving connection between friends, but can also show captivity. Dog collars and handcuffs both indicate subservience to an authority. Wedding rings, class rings, and the white collars of priests demonstrate a voluntary link with another being or entity. In India, placing metallic circles around the body—as when wearing bangles—is believed to protect one from evil spirits.

Circularity has ancient meaning, partly because of the many spheres and ovoids found in nature. From the mega-circles traced by the earth, moon and planets as they orbit the sun, to the micro-spheroids of seeds and eggs, the basic shape of nature is round. Babies gestate while enclosed in jug-shaped wombs, and birds keep hatchlings safe in rounded nests. A circle is used in biological diagrams to demonstrate the cycle of life.

The religious power of the disk is recognized by many cultures and manifested around the world. That ancient rock paintings of "sun wheels" pre-date the invention of the actual wheel indicates the archetypal nature of this shape. Neolithic people *felt* something about it, and archetypes, as defined by Jung and von Franz, are as much about the emotion behind something as the thing itself. What the people seemed to have felt was the completeness, or wholeness, of the circle.

The term *omphalos* is a Greek word meaning "the naval of the universe," and refers to the center point of all known things, the divine. The earliest people of the British Isles built *cromlechs,* which are cairns, or circular piles of stones with spiritual significance. Megalithic circles, such as Stonehenge and Avebury, were carefully planned and erected to coordinate with the looping celestial movements. Women in ancient Mexico wore snail-shell amulets during childbirth. Their belief was that the animal's easy slide from under its spiral shell would allow their own baby to follow a similar gentle emergence. The early Egyptians worshipped the sun god Ra, who was represented by a disk with rays reaching down and ending in human hands. In South America, the Incas used round stones and sunflowers in ceremonies invoking their solar god.

Wheels are circles that provide transportation, and thus, power. A person who has a vehicle can go farther than one without. We travel on land with wheels and we use them to measure our passage through time. The lunar calendars used to mark the Jewish and Muslim years are circular, as was that of the Aztecs. The Gregorian calendar of the West is sometimes shown as a wheel. The animal signs of the Eastern zodiac are a cycle that takes twelve years to complete.

The "wheel of life" is iconic of Buddhism. Brahma, the Indian creator of the universe, stood on a "huge, thousand pointed lotus," which is a flower evocative of a wheel. He gazed in each of the four directions of the compass, and his line of sight traced a circle. This was his preparation for creating all that would be contained within it. Siddhartha Gautama, the Buddha, was born somewhere in the Himalayan mountains and, at that moment, a lotus flower is said to have sprung from the earth, its array of eight petals representing the totality of the being just arrived. His *dharma*, or teachings, concerned the cyclic nature of existence. Birth, life, death, and rebirth follow one after the other in the journey towards *nirvana*, or enlightenment.

Mandala, the Hindu word for circle, describes sacred visual representations of the human mind. Dr. Carl Jung used mandalas to illustrate the "nuclear atom of the human psyche." The Navajo American Indians create mandalas in ceremonies to aid in balancing mental processes; in Eastern culture they are tools for meditation and self-awareness.

The Christian prophet Ezekiel described his vision of the cherubim as being accompanied by wheels "that sparkled like chrysolite." Each wheel "appeared to be made like a wheel intersecting a wheel...their rims were high and awesome, and all four rims were full of eyes all around." The wheels went wherever the angels did and were said to have contained their spirit. (Ezekiel 1:10-14)

The Greek word *temenos* means a circle enclosing a sacred space; one who stays within its bounds is said to be safe from harm. It stems from the verb *temno,* meaning "to cut." In the Hindu classic poem the *Ramayana*, Rama's wife Sita is literally circumscribed to keep her safe from demons. When she steps beyond the boundary drawn in the soil outside her hut, she is kidnapped by *Rakshasas,* or demons. In Jewish tradition, Honi the sage prays for rain, but his pleas are answered only after he repeats them from within a circle he has drawn in the dust.

Such circles need not be truly sacred. They can be simply an area cut off from other places for a special purpose. When mothers and fathers embrace their children with their arms, for safety or to express love, they create a protected circle. Burrowing animals dig circular dens for safe retreat. Territorial mammals, including human beings, feel most secure in the center of their territory. The circus ring where acts are performed or a sports arena where ball games are played are traditionally circular. In both places, fans sit in rings of seating to watch, creating concentric circles around an inner ring, where the power is concentrated. That sports teams enjoy a home town advantage has been documented, showing us that this phenomenon is still present in the twenty-first century.

Ceremonial food is often circular. The traditional western wedding cake, with its stacked, concentric circles is the most obvious contemporary American example. Round food is often joyful: think birthday cupcakes and Sunday morning stacks of hotcakes. The Chinese eat small round "moon cakes" to celebrate the harvest moon and the coming to earth of Cheng-O, the Moon Lady; Mexican wedding cookies are rounds of nuts and meringue.

Rings in fairy tales often carry power, and they are sometimes inscribed with runes or other writings. Historic engraved rings, such as the Kingmoor Ring dug from the ground near Greymoor Hill in England in 1817, may be echoes of fairy tale jewelry. Such a real-life "ring of power" may have inspired J.R.R. Tolkien when he wrote *The Lord of the Rings* trilogy in 1963. Modern day wedding rings, etched with the date of marriage and the initials of the bride and groom, are powerful reminders of a ring's potent symbolism.

In Cinderella stories where they appear, rings are a token by which the girl is recognized. Sometimes the jewelry is surreptitiously slipped onto Cinderella's finger as she dances with the prince, and he recognizes her by it later. In other stories, she is the one who deliberately drops a ring into a loaf of bread dough or dish of soup, knowing that the prince will find it. In one Cinderella story from India, *Anklet for a Princess: A Cinderella Story from India*, by Meredith Babeaux Brucker and Lila Mehta (2002), it is Godfather Snake who provides the girl with diamond-studded anklets to wear to the festival. When she loses one on the way home, the prince seeks and eventually finds her, by means of the matching anklet she still wears. Her dance for him, using the circular movements she learned from her mother, convinces him that she is a true princess.

Gioachino Rossini chose to use a golden bracelet in his opera version of Cinderella, *La Cenerentola*. This 1817 comedic opera involves an elaborate series of switched identifies, as Don Ramiro, Prince of Salerno, changes places with his tutor, Alidoro. His valet Dandini masquerades as the prince, and Cinderella, who falls in love with Ramiro while he is dressed as a servant, gives him one of her pair of golden bracelets. Later, when he has revealed his true identity, he recognizes her by it and makes her his wife.

Shoes

Shoes play an important role in our lives, and they have played important roles in history. Clothing is one of the fundamental needs of people, and the earliest humans figured out how to protect their feet by wrapping reeds and grass around them. American Indians and others discovered the process of tanning leather. They first tied pieces of it on to their feet with leather strings, and later figured out how to sew elaborate moccasins. These were sometimes decorated with beads, feathers, and porcupine quills, and were used by many tribes to show rank.

For much of history, owning shoes depended largely on geography and social status. In tropical regions, many people simply went barefoot most of the time. In some areas sandals were worn by everyone, including soldiers and kings, at rest and in battle. King Tutankhamun of Egypt took his throne at the age of nine in the year 1361 B.C.E.

When he was a teenager, he ordered the images of his enemies to be painted onto the soles of his sandals, so that he could walk on them with every step.

In Biblical times, when two men made a business contract, they did not sign their names on a piece of paper. Instead, the buyer took off one of his sandals and gave it to the seller of the property. People who witnessed one man giving a shoe to another could be called to testify that a deal had taken place.

The Greeks gods, in their splendid home on Mount Olympus, are shown wearing tunics and sandals. But only one had wings on his so that he could travel swiftly. This was Hermes, the trickster god, whom the Romans called Mercury. The child of Zeus and Maia, Hermes was mischievous even when he was a brand-new baby. One story tells how he sneaked out of his cradle and stole cows from his big brother, Apollo. He sacrificed two of the herd, but kept their intestines to make strings for a musical instrument he had just invented, the lyre. Baby Hermes then played a tune, hid the cows and snuck back into his cradle before anyone knew what he had done. When his father found out, Hermes soothed him with music and gave the cows back to Apollo. Zeus rewarded his son's cleverness with a pair of winged sandals that could carry him across the world in an instant. The youth became a messenger and was revered as the god of those who are nimble and swift of foot and mind, including merchants, travelers and thieves.

In cold climates, not having shoes meant that one might freeze to death simply by going outside of the house. Boots and leather shoes were expensive because they took a lot of time to make, so many people did without, or wore the cast offs of others. Sometimes poor people carved shoes out of wood to make clogs. Since those who had servants did not need to wear such sturdy footwear, nobles often wore soft slippers of wool or silk. During the Middle Ages, from about the fourth through the fourteenth centuries, some people wore wooden platforms called *pattons* to keep their stockings off the dirt floors.

By the fifth century, the fashion among wealthy Europeans was to wear shoes that stuck far out in front of the toes and curled up to a point. As long ago as 950 C.E. people in Norway and other parts of Northern Europe had figured out how to attach blades to the bottoms of their shoes so that they could skate on ice.

In China, the aristocracy developed the custom of women wearing very small shoes. It was considered to be a sign of both beauty and wealth, as the ladies who could wear the tiny slippers were not able to walk or even to move around very much. They had to have servants to help them with everything. Those small feet came at a terrible cost: at about the age of six, well-born girls had their toes broken and folded under the foot. The arch was sometimes snapped as well, and then wrappings were bound tightly around to prevent growth. This allowed women to wear slippers no bigger than four inches long.

Clearly, a woman who had been crippled in this

way could not earn a living or take care of herself. She was completely reliant on her husband, making foot binding a way of claiming ownership of her.

Shoes and marriage rituals are intertwined in many cultures with less extreme versions of dependence. One wedding tradition in Anglo-Saxon England involved the bride's father passing her shoes to the new husband, showing a transfer of responsibility. The symbolism of a foot sliding into a shoe can represent the relationship between husband and wife. According to a Jungian interpretation, a foot so inserted represents the sex act, and implies that the father, by handing over her shoes, consents to his daughter's sexual maturity. In contemporary times, a remnant of this custom is the practice of tying old shoes to the bumper of the bride and groom's car.

There are many superstitions involving shoes. Among the Omaha American Indian tribe, there is a belief that cutting a hole in the sole of a sick child's moccasin promotes healing. This is said to prevent the little one from following the spirit of death to the underworld because his shoes are too worn out for the journey. There is a similar folk custom in England that says one can predict whether a sick person will live or die by throwing a shoe over their house. Whether it lands sole up or sole down decrees their prognosis.

In the Philippines, it is considered back luck to leave your bedroom slippers far apart from one another, lest spirits take one, and in many parts of the world putting your left shoe on first is believed to be unlucky. Queen Victoria of England, who reigned from 1837 to 1901, wrote in her private journal about moving into the royal residence at Balmoral, Scotland. Her servants, she noted with satisfaction, threw an old shoe in before she entered, to bring her good luck.

Ancient customs connecting footwear with the celebration of Christmas continue to this day in many parts of the world. One is the hanging of stockings, or decorated socks, by the fireplace on December 24th so that they can be filled with gifts and candy. In the United States, it is said to be Santa Claus who fills them, in England it is Father Christmas. Another practice dates to the 4th century, when a man named Nicholas lived in Turkey. He saved children from poverty and eventually became a bishop. In some Eastern European countries, children still put their shoes out and wait for Saint Nicholas to come on December 6th, which is his saint's day. They hope that his helper, Black Peter, is not with him, because he is the one who carries a switch and a list of children who have been bad. In Spain and Italy they say that the Three Kings will leave fruit or candy in children's shoes on the night of January 6th.

A common fairy tale motif for men involves a taboo against stepping foot on the ground lest it break a spell. In Ireland, the warrior poet Oisin is said to have gone to Tir Na Nog, the land of the fairies, with beautiful Niam. When he wished to visit home, she let him, though she warned that he must not dismount from his horse. He does, and ages a thousand years in an instant.

The English fairy tale of King Herla, who invites the elf king to his wedding, has the same message. Herla goes to the land of elves and has a wonderful visit. Before he returns home, he is given a blood-hound small enough to hold in his hand. The elf king warns him that he must not dismount from his horse before the little dog has touched the ground. But at the crucial moment, Herla is distracted and forgets. The instant his foot touches the ground he disintegrates into dust. His horse returns alone to Tir Na Nog.

Fairy tale shoes sometimes bring good fortune. In another Grimm tale, elves surprised the old shoe-maker who was down to his last piece of leather. They stitched him such a fine pair of shoes that he got a high price for them, and so could buy more hide. Each day the cobbler marked and cut out pieces. Each night the elves sewed them up so beautifully that the old man became rich. In thanks, he made several pairs of tiny shoes, and his wife made little suits of clothing, which they left for the elves. After that, "the shoe-maker continued to be prosperous until the end of his life and succeeded in all his endeavors."

In the story *Puss in Boots*, a miller with three sons dies. The oldest son gets the mill, the middle inherits the donkey, and the youngest gets the cat. This cat pleads to have a pair of boots made in his size, and the man agrees. Wearing the boots and a cape, the cat begins a series of trades. Starting with a sack of grain, he ends by tricking everyone into believing that his master is the "Marquis of Carabas." In this guise, the young man becomes friends with the king and marries the princess. Some versions of this tale cast the cat as female.

Women's shoes of legend and lore are rarely designed for athletics. More often, they are of very odd sizes or unusual materials. They may be huge, like that of the Old Woman who actually lived in a shoe. It was, according to ancient rhyme, big enough to house "so many children she didn't know what to do." The shoes may be tiny, as the shoe of the first-century Chinese Cinderella, Yeh-hsien, must have been. They may be made of unforgiving material such as gold, silver, diamonds, or glass, or they may be wooden clodhoppers. The twelve princesses who danced through the soles of their shoes every night, on secret escapades with twelve princes, clearly had a problem with their slippers.

Sometimes being able to fit into a shoe is really important. Becoming a princess, and leaving behind a life of hard work, cold feet and an empty belly is a pretty strong motivator. In many Cinderella stories the stepsisters are so jealous of Cinderella when she wears the slippers that they plot revenge. In the Vietnamese tale of *Kajong and Halœk*, they lure her up a tree to pick coconuts, then chop it down when she is high on the trunk. In the American *Ashpet*, they take her for a picnic and then abandon her on an island with the Hairy Man, who tries to drown her.

Jacob and Wilhelm Grimm collected a local folk tale in 1812 called *Aschenputtel*, or *Cinderfoot*. In that story, the mistreated girl gets her ball gown and golden shoes from a bird in a tree. When the prince lays a tar-trap on the palace steps, she loses a shoe while running away. He undertakes a search to find the mysterious girl who came to his ball, using the shoe as a test of identity. In their desperation to wear it, her stepsisters cut off part of their own feet with a knife. This is not so very different from the mutilation done to poor little rich girls in China, or from modern day women who wear "ankle-breakers"– shoes with stiletto heels.

Magic shoes play a role in the twentieth-century fairy tale *The Wizard of Oz*. Written by L. Frank Baum in 1900, it was to be the first in a series of more than a dozen books about his magical land. The story opens with Dorothy, a Kansas farm girl who lives in a tiny house, "with the great, gray prairie on every side." She is an orphan, cared for by her Aunt Em, a woman who is "thin and gaunt and never smiles." Her Uncle Henry is a farmer whose work never ends. Baum tells us that the man "did not know what joy was."

When Dorothy and her dog Toto are caught up in a cyclone, they land in Oz. Right on top of the Wicked Witch of the East, as it turns out. Oz is a land of beauty and color, peopled by many kind and amusing citizens. The local council of Munchkins gives Dorothy the witch's silver shoes as a reward for killing that villain. Ultimately, the shoes, which are charmed, carry her home. The ones that Judy Garland so famously wore as Dorothy in the 1939 film version were enhanced, becoming ruby slippers.

Gregory McGuire's 1995 *Wicked: The Life and Times of the Wicked Witch of the West* also features silver shoes worn by both Elphaba and her sister, Nessarose.

Spinning Wheels, Spindles, and Looms

Prior to the invention of spinning and weaving, people either went naked or used animal skins to cover themselves. Learning to make cloth was a major human accomplishment. When we think of all of the kinds of fabric that we use, and then imagine life without them, the true value of textiles becomes clear. From blankets and rugs to socks and towels, cloth plays a critical role in the comfort and health of humanity.

Looms and spindles from archeological excavations have been dated as early as the Neolithic era, when clay *spindle whorls* were used to spin clumps of animal hair into rough twine. Spindle whorls were small cone-shaped devices that were held in the hand.

The basic process of spinning thread and weaving it into cloth varies only slightly depending upon whether one is spinning short fibers, such as sheep's wool, or longer ones, such as flax or silk. It is a time-consuming process that begins with gathering the rough material and preparing it for spinning. If wool cloth is desired, first sheep must be raised and sheared. The fleece is then *carded*, or combed to remove impurities and to align the fibers. Then bits of it are spun around rapidly, causing the fibers to stretch and twist around one another. The thread is made longer by adding new tufts on the end and stretching them into place.

Flax, which provides the fibers for making linen, is one of mankind's oldest cultivated plants. Stored seeds have been found in Syria and Turkey and carbon dated to 7,000 B.C. E. As early as 5,000 B.C.E. the Egyptians were farming it on a large-scale basis. By the 1st century C.E., France and Belgium were European centers of linen production, a complex, multi-step process. Flax seeds produce blue or white flowers on tall, slender stalks. These are then soaked and pounded to remove the soft outer layer of the stem. The remaining fibers are beaten into a soft mass, and bits then drawn out and spun. A bundle of flax or other fibers ready for spinning was called *tow*.

The "queen of fibers" is silk. One cocoon of the moth *Bombix mori* can produce a filament one thousand yards long. Many of these filaments must be wound together before they can be spun into thread, making silk extremely strong as well as lustrous. Silk is the stuff of legend and has provided luxurious robes for royalty since ancient times. The Chinese discovered that mulberry-leaf eating caterpillars wound themselves into silky pods before emerging as large moths. Silk thread is attributed to an empress in 2700 B.C.E. who dropped a pod into her tea and was astounded at the length and near invisibility of the thread she pulled from it.

Silk production was a closely guarded Chinese secret until the middle of the 1st century. That's when the Roman emperor Justinian succeeded in having two of his men smuggle out some moths. Disguised as monks, they carried their prize out of China in hollowed bamboo tubes.

It is thought that the mechanical device for winding silk filaments was the forerunner of the spinning wheel. That contraption is powered by working a foot pedal, much like a modern sewing machine, and was invented during the 12th century.

The tools used for making thread vary somewhat according to region and the fiber being spun, but the basic equipment is the same. These include a *spindle,* which is a stick of wood that is about a foot long and pointed on one end. Another kind of spindle is the pin connecting the doorknobs on either side of a door. The warning sometimes printed on checks and official documents, "Do not fold, spindle, or mutilate," refers to the practice of using a vertically held pin over which notes are thrust. They are then held in place by the spindle that pierces them. In the fairy tale now known as *Sleeping Beauty*, the princess pricks her finger on a tool for spinning thread.

Fibers are wrapped around the pointed end of a spindle, which is then twirled with one hand. The other hand is needed to feed fluff into the growing length of thread. In some cultures, women dangle the spindle like a whirling yo-yo, leaving one hand free to push fibers and the other to keep drawing out thread.

In some areas a distaff was used. The word comes from the ancient English word *dis*, which meant fibers, and *staff*, which is simply a long stick. Thus a *distaff* is a big stick upon which the raw fibers for spinning were wrapped.

A *bobbin* is the spool around which the finished thread is wound. This word also describes part of a modern sewing machine, the small wheel of thread that feeds up from the bottom to meet the needle coming down from the top.

Tools for spinning and weaving were often buried with women, as weapons and other items were buried with men. Tombs from the Bronze Age (2000 B.C.E.), have been discovered to contain spindles made of silver and gold. Historic references to such precious metal implements used by noble ladies or given to one another as gifts are many. Homer's *Odyssey* describes an Egyptian lady sending gifts to Helen of Troy. They included a golden spindle and a silver-edged basket for storing wool.

Such tools were not trinkets or decorative baubles: there is ample historic evidence showing that noblewomen did not delegate all of the spinning to their maids, but engaged in the task themselves.

Weaving cloth fell to the lady of the house, and it takes a great deal of thread to weave a yard of fabric. All available hands were needed for the task, but differences in the raw material were important. In a world of earth tones, brightly colored dye was reserved for royalty. Princesses and queens spun skeins of wool dyed purple with the shells of sea snails, or wove linen cloth into which they threaded golden beads.

Women of all social strata spent the better part of their waking hours spinning and weaving. By about 500 B.C.E. they had figured out how to weave complex patterns, including herringbone and twill. Fragments of these have been recovered from sites in the Austrian Alps and can be seen at the Natural History Museum in Vienna today.

There are textile historians who believe that the famous marble statue of Venus de Milo, who is missing her arms, was originally depicted in the act of spinning. The shoulders and torso of the statute are in the very position in which women in Greece held their spindle and distaff, as superimposition of these tools has shown.

Weaving is the process by which thread is made into cloth. Before weaving can begin, thread must be bound to a *loom* to form the base upon which other threads will be crossed. This base of vertical threads is called the *weft*. The threads that pass over it are called the *warp*.

Looms can be quite large wooden structures, as in Navajo, European, and Japanese weaving. Some cultures developed small, portable looms that could be strapped around the waist, such as the backstrap looms used by the Aztecs and Mayas. Women in South and Central America used the abundant cactus in their craft. They spun thread from its fibers on spindles made out of spines.

Greek ladies used an entirely different kind of

loom, one that was *warp weighted*. Suspended from a beam, the warp threads were held down with large beads on the ends to pull them straight.

The trio of Greek goddesses known as the Fates were said to have the responsibility for the duration and form of each human existence. Klotho was the one who "spun the thread of life," Lachesia held it and measured its length, and Atropos snipped the thread, marking the death of an individual. The word *span*, still in common use to describe the length of a lifetime, comes originally from the past tense of the verb *to spin, or draw out.*

The making of textiles, by nature of its complex designs and level of skill, carries power and has long been associated with magic and spiritualism. Many cultures connect the creation of thread with the creation of life or geological events. The Maya Rainbow Lady, Ixchel, was their goddess of childbirth and is always shown weaving.

In Japanese folklore, they say that the King of the Sky was quite proud of his daughter, the Weaving Princess. Her fabric was "so light and airy, so thin and smooth, that it was hung among the stars in the sky and draped toward the earth," the origin of clouds and mist.

Ceremonies, such as those performed by the Navajo American Indians before they begin to weave, are found in every culture where women have made cloth. The Navajo perform a corn pollen ceremony at sunrise, in which the powder is brushed onto the head, into the mouth, and in the direction of the sun. They send prayers remembering Changing Woman, who learned to dye wool using ground abalone shells and various plants. According to legend, she learned to weave from Spider Woman, who taught her always to weave in a white thread in one part of the border. This was to give the weaver "an escape from the middle of the blanket" because to seal the pattern meant that "you will close in your life and thoughts." The Navajo weave geometric patterns or images of the natural world into their rugs.

In Egypt and Mesopotamia, special patterns were woven into fabrics to denote rank or for use in rituals such as weddings or births. Ancient Egyptian tunics have been found with the ankh, symbol of long life, woven into the neck and sleeves.

Numerology, a widely practiced form of divination, shows up in some weaving patterns. An intricate striped cloth from the Bronze Age Netherlands uses a mathematical pattern found in the runic alphabet. Its discovery marks the possibility of a real-life magic cloth of the kind that are so common in fairy tales.

A clearer example of the power of the woven pattern is depicted in Homer's *Iliad*. During the height of the Trojan War, Princess Andromache begins weaving a special cloak for her husband, Hector. The thread count of the rose pattern was meant to protect him, but he is killed before the cloak is finished.

The weaving of tapestries, in which the weft threads are actually wound around those of the warp to cover them, is a specialized craft. France and Belgium during the 12th through 16th centuries were the world centers of the wool tapestry works. The heavy rugs were hung on the walls of stone castles to provide insulation.

For millennia, spinning and weaving were such a part of daily life that it is hardly a surprise to find references to it in folk and fairy tales. The earliest recorded European tale involving a girl who is thrust into a deep slumber by means of a spindle is that of *Sun, Moon, and Talia.* This is diversion number five on the fifth day of Basile's *Il Pentamerone.* Here the daughter of "a great lord" is foretold to be under the threat of danger due to a "chip of flax." Although her father bans spinning of any kind in the castle, the girl observes an old woman spinning as she walks down the street, passing by under her window. Of course Talia begs to try her hand at this unfamiliar task, and a splinter of flax pricks her finger. She falls dead to the ground and is revived only when it is removed by accident, many years later. In the version collected by the Grimm Brothers in 1812, *Little Briar Rose,* it is the kiss of a prince who revives the Sleeping Beauty after she has been similarly injured.

Spinning wheels play a significant role in the story of *Rumpelstiltskin*, where a girl must spin straw into gold. A wicked dwarf does the job for her but only on condition that the young lady give him her first born child when it arrives. In despair she makes the promise, but is later able to win her child back by guessing the little man's name.

Lesser known Grimm's tales include *Spindle, Needle, Shuttle*, and *The Three Spinners*.

In Cinderella stories, spinning wheels, spindles, and bobbins are usually found in the Catskin variant. In this type of story, Cinderella's mother gives her golden trinkets before she dies, telling her that they will help her when she is in need. These items are usually a gold ring, a tiny spinning wheel, and a gold or silver bobbin. Often, they fit into a magic nutshell that provides the girl with dresses for the ball. When Catskin is asked to make either soup or bread for the prince, she slips one of her golden trinkets into the dish. It is by this token of recognition that she is later identified.

Notes on the Stories

Story Number One: Cinderella

This story is based on Charles Perrault's *Cinderilla or the Little Glass Slipper* as published by Iona & Peter Opie in *The Classic Fairy Tales* (1974), Oxford University Press. That book contains twenty-four of the most famous fairy tales as they were first printed in the English language, with original spelling and punctuation.

It is also based on C. Betts (2009) & C. Perrault (1697) *Histoires ou contes du temps passé avec des moralités: Contes de ma mère l'Oye or Histories, or tales of past times; with morals: Mother goose tales. Complete fairy tales of Charles Perrault: A new translation.* Oxford University Press. I have tried to retain accuracy in story details while enhancing clarity so that the story can serve as a base for better comprehension of other Cinderella stories.

Story Number Two:
Cinderilla or the Little Glass Slipper

This story is also based on the Charles Perrault story featured in Iona & Peter Opies' 1974 *The classic fairy tales*, Oxford University Press, and on C. Betts. (2009) & C. Perrault, (1697) *Histoires ou contes du temps passé avec des moralités: Contes de ma mère l'Oye or Histories, or tales of past times; with morals: Mother goose tales. Complete fairy tales of Charles Perrault: A new translation.* Oxford University Press.

This is the source of the glass slippers and the pumpkin coach. Animal helpers are the mice that are transformed into horses, the rat who becomes a coachman, and the lizards that are Cinderilla's footmen. The story uses a pumpkin as the vehicle for travelling to the balls, and a fairy godmother to grant wishes. Cinderilla attends three balls where the prince falls in love with her, loses a glass slipper at the palace, and is later identified when she can fit that shoe. She then produces its mate and all recognize her as the beauty from the ball.

Story Number Three: Aschenputtel

This is the German folktale collected by the Brothers Grimm and published in 1812 in their first collection, *Kinder und Hausmarchen (Children's and Household Tales)*. It was translated by Jack Zipes and is included in *The Complete Fairy Tales of the Brothers Grimm* (2003) New York: Bantam Books. In that book, Zipes gives the title as *Cinderella*. But in his 2000 book *The Oxford com-*

panion to fairy tales (Oxford University Press), he retains her German name, *Aschenputtel*. I have chosen to use that name to emphasize the German origin of the story.

There is no fairy godmother and no pumpkin.

Animal helpers in *Aschenputtel* are birds, including pigeons and turtledoves. They sort the lentils from the ash for her so that she can go to the ball, and then throw down dresses and shoes for her to wear. When she flees the prince, she hides from him in her father's dovecote, but he chops it down. The doves also alert the prince to the stepsister's bleeding feet when they try to fool him and wear the shoe though it does not fit.

Aschenputtel also has a helper in the form of a plant: the hazel twig that she asks her father to bring home grows into a tree, which attracts the doves in the first place.

The girl attends three balls and is identified when she is able to wear the shoe brought by the prince's servant. In this tale, the stepmother encourages her own daughters to cut off parts of their feet so that they can wear the shoe, and at the end, her father is responsible for allowing her to try the shoe on. It is a bloody story with a gory ending: the wicked stepsisters are blinded by doves as punishment for their cruelty to Aschenputtel.

Other Grimms Fairy Tales that are very similar to *Aschenputtel* and feature many identifying marks of Cinderella stories include *Bearskin; The Old Woman in the Forest; One Eye, Two Eyes, and Three Eyes*, and *Spindle, Shuttle, and Needle*.

Story Number Four: Catskins

This story was taken from folklorist Richard Chase's 1948 *Grandfather Tales: American-English Folktales*. New York: Houghton Mifflin Company. He describes collecting the tale during a trip to Kentucky, and emphasizes the oral nature of story telling. Chase said in his forward:

> Filling up blank paper is, indeed, not the same as the sound of your own voice shaping a tale as it wells up out of your memory and as your own fancy plays with all its twists and turns...After you have learned the tales in silent print, shut the book and tell 'em!

Chase recorded this story in mountain dialect, but I have followed his advice and substituted common speech so that the meaning of the story does not get lost in misunderstanding some of the words. Nevertheless, I have tried to retain the mountain feeling in my version. I have set it in North Carolina because of an interesting connection I learned of with the legendary backwoodsman, Daniel Boone. He single handedly explored much of North Carolina, Tennessee, and Kentucky, and was a first generation American, born in Pennsylvania in 1735. His parents emigrated from England, so perhaps he grew up hearing the English version of *Catskin*. (That story can be found in Earnest Rhys' 1906 *A Book of Old English Fairy Tales: Fairy Gold*. Reprinted 2008 New York: Dover Publications Inc.)

Story Number Five: Chinye

This story is based in part on Obi Oneyfulu's 1994 *Chinye: A West African Folktale*. I also used fragmented descriptions of it found on www.thinkquest.org. Additionally, I used African folktale motifs including magic gourds, a wise woman who lives near the water, and the prosocial values of sharing the wealth with one's community. African folk tales which contributed ideas to this story include *Oniyeye and King Olu Dotun's Daughter*, and *The Sacred Milk of Koumongoe*, both found in Kevin Crossley-Holland's 1998 *The Young Oxford Book of Fairy Tales*. Oxford University Press.

Bibliography

Arbuthnot, M.H. & Wright, B.F. (1916/1988) *The real Mother Goose*. Chicago: Rand McNally & Co.

Anderson, H.C. (1983) *The complete tales and stories*. New York: Anchor Books

Angeli, de, M. *Marguerite de Angeli's book of nursery and Mother Goose rhymes*. (1953) New York: Doubleday Inc.

Ashe, G. (1990) *Mythology of the British Isles*. London: Guild Publishing

Babbit, E.C. (1912) *Jataka tales: Animal stories*. New York: Appleton-Century-Crofts

Barber, E. W. (1994) *Women's work: The first 20,000 years: Women, cloth, and society in early times*. New York: W.W. Norton

Barrie, J. M. (1911) *Peter Pan*. New York: Signet

Base, G. (1996) *The discovery of dragons: New research revealed*. New York: Harry N. Abrams

Basile, G. *Il pentamerone* (Trans. Burton, R., K.C., M. G. 1637/1943) New York: Liveright

Baum, L.F. (1900) *The wonderful wizard of Oz*. Chicago: The Reilly and Lee Co.

Belting, N. M. (1961) *Elves and ellefolk: Tales of the little people.* New York: Holt, Rinehart & Winston Inc.

Bettelheim, B. (1975) *The uses of enchantment: The meaning and importance of fairy tales.* New York: Alfred A. Knopf.

Betts, C. (2009) Perrault, C. (1697) *Histoires ou contes du temps passé avec des moralités: Contes de ma mère l'Oye or HIstories, or tales of past times; with morals: Mother goose tales. Complete fairy tales of Charles Perrault: A new translation.* Oxford University Press

Bleandonu, G. (2006) Trans. Leighton, S. *What do children dream?* London: Free Association Books ISBN 1-84353-729-8, www.fabooks.com.

Bol, M.C. (Ed., 1998) *Stars above, earth below: American Indians and nature.* Colorado: Roberts Rinehart

Browning, R. (1998) *The Pied Piper of Hamelin.* Australia: Angus and Robertson Children's

Bruchac, J. & Ross, G. (1994). *The girl who married the moon: Tales from Native North America.* Bride Water Books

Bullfinch, T. *Bullfinch's mythology.* (1855/1969) New York: Avenel Books

Burgess, G. (1915/1961) *The Purple Cow.* New York: Dover

Brucker, M.B. & Mehta, L. (2002) *Anklet for a princess: A Cinderella story from India*. CA: Shen's

Bryan, A. (1971) *The ox of the wonderful horns and other African folktales*. New York: Atheneum

Carpenter, F. (1937) *Tales of a Chinese grandmother*. New York: Doubleday & Company, Inc.

Calvino, I. (1956/1980) *Italian Folktales: Selected and retold*. New York: Harcourt Brace

Carr-Gomm, R. & Heygate, R. *The book of English magic*. (2009) New York: The Overlook Press

Carrol, L. (1865/2011) *Alice in wonderland* and *Through the looking glass*. USA: Tribeca Books

Cassidy, J., Valadez, C.M., & Garret, S.D. (2010, May) Literacy trends and issues: A look at the five pillars and the cement that supports them. *The Reading Teacher: A Journal of Research-Based Classroom Practice* 63 (8) 644-655.

Chase, R. (1948/1976) *Grandfather tales: American-English folktales*. New York: Hougton Mifflin Company.

Cleary, B. (1970) *Runaway Ralph*. New York: Morrow Junior Books

Cook, J., Kramer, A. & Rowland-Entwhistle (1981) *History's timeline: A forty thousand year chronology of civilizations*. New York: Crescent Books

Cothrann, J. (1956) *The magic calabash: More folk tales from America's islands and Alaska*. New York: David McCay Company, Inc.

Cox, M.R. *(1892/2010) Cinderella: Three hundred forty-five variants of Cinderella, Catskin, and Cap O'Rushes*. New York: Cornell Digital Library. www.library.cornell.edu

Creech, S. (1994). *Walk two moons*. New York: HarperTrophy

Crossley-Holland (1998) *The young Oxford book of fairy tales*. Oxford University Press

Davison, G. M. (2000) *Tales from the Taiwanese*. Connecticut/London: Libraries Unlimited

Delacre, L. (1996) *Golden tales: Myths, legends, and folktales from Latin America*. New York: Scholastic Press

El-Shamy, H. M. *Folktales of Egypt, collected, translated and edited, with Middle Eastern and African parallels*. (1980) The University of Chicago Press

English National Opera Guide (1980) *La Cenerentola (Cinderella) Rossini*. London: Calder

Finch, C. *The art of Walt Disney: From Mickey Mouse to the magic kingdom* (1975) Burbank, CA: Walt Disney Productions

Freud, S. (2001) *On dreams*. New York: Dover

Folklore Society, www.folklore-society.com

Gannet, R. S. (1948/2008) *My father's dragon*. New York: Random House

Grahame, K. (1908) *The wind in the willows*. New York: Grosset & Dunlap

Gobble, P. (1998) *The legend of the Buffalo Woman*. Washington D.C.: National Geographic Society

Hamilton, E. (1942) *Mythology*. New York: Little, Brown and Company

Hamilton, V. (1985). *The people could fly: American black folktales*. New York: Alfred A. Knopf

Hamlyn, P. (1973) *New Larousse encyclopedia of mythology*. London: Author

Haviland, V. (1966) *Favorite fairy tales told in Czechoslovakia*. Boston: Little, Brown and Company

Haviland, V. (1971) *Favorite fairy tales told in Greece*. Boston: Little, Brown and Company

Haycock, K. & Jerald, C. (2002) Closing the Achievement Gap. *Principal* (Reston, VA) 82 (2) 6-11. Retrieved from http://vnweb.hwwilsonweb.com

Heibert, E. & Fisher, C. (2005) A review of the national reading panel's studies on fluency: The role of text. *The Elementary School Journal* 105 (5) Doi: 10.1086431888

Herodotus, trans. 1954

Hickox, R. (1998) *The golden sandal*. New York: Holiday House

Hunt, M. *(trans. 1968) Grimm's fairy tales* Chicago: Follett

Jacobs, J. (1891) *More Celtic fairy tales*. New York: G. P. Putnam's Sons.

Jacobs, J. (1916) *European folk and fairy tales*. New York: G. P. Putnam's Sons.

Jackson, (1952) *The tawny, scrawny lion*. New York: Golden Books

Jacques, B. (1988) *Redwall* (series) New York: Avon Books

Jaffrey, M. (1985) *Seasons of splendour: Tales, myths & legends of India*. New York: Atheneum. Holliday, L.

Jones, A. (1995). *Larousse dictionary of world folklore*. New York: Larousse

Jung, Henderson, Jaffé, A., Jacobi, & von Franz, (1964) *Man and his symbols*. New York, NY: Doubleday.

Kraus, R. (1971) *Leo the late bloomer*. New York: HarperCollins Children's Books

Kipling, R. (1935) *The just so stories*. New York: Weathervane Books

Lair, D. *The ogress and the snake and other stories from Somalia*. (2009) London: Frances Lincoln

Lantzgoldenagecartoons.com

Leaf, M. (1937/2007) *The story of Ferdinand*. New York: Puffin Storytime

Lear, E. (1991) *The owl and the pussycat illustrated by Brett, J.* New York: Putnam and Grosset

Lewis, C. S. (1950/ 1994) *The chronicles of Narnia*. New York: HarperTrophy

Lillard, A. (2007) *Montessori: The science behind the genius*. Oxford University Press

Lobel, A. (1970) *Frog and Toad are friends*. New York: HarperCollins

Louie, A.I. (1982) *Yeh-Shen: A Cinderella story from China*. London: Puffin Books.

Maguire, G. (1995) *Wicked: The life and times of The Wicked Witch of the West*. New York: Harper.

Manguel, A. & Guadalupi, G. *The dictionary of imaginary places*. (2000) San Diego/New York/London: Harcourt Books

Manheim, R. (1983) *Kinder- und haus marchen (Household tales for young and old by Jacob and Wilhelm Grimm)* New York: Anchor

Masao, S. & Kojima, S. (2001) *Vietnamese tales of rabbits and watermelons*. CA: Heian

McCall, H. (2002) *Gods and goddesses of the ancient Egyptians*. New York: Peter Bedrick

McCloskey, R. (1941) *Make way for ducklings*. New York: The Viking Press

McMaster, G. & Trafzer, C.E. (Eds., 2004) *Native universe: Voices of American Indians*. Washington, D.C.: National Geographic Society

Meyer, M. (1975) *A boy, a dog. and a frog*. New York: Dial

Meyer, M. & Willaims, J. (1984) *Everyone knows what a dragon looks like*. New York: Aladdin

Milne, A. A. (1926/1994) *The complete tales of Winnie the Pooh*. New York: L.P. Dutton

O'Brien, R., (1971) *Mrs. Frisby and the rats of NIMH*. New York: Simon & Schuster

Onyefulu, O. (1994) *Chinye: A West African folk-tale*. New York: Penguin Books USA Inc.

Opie, I. & Opie, P. (1974) *The classic fairy tales*. Oxford University Press

Osborne, M. P. *American tall tales* (1991) New York: Alfred A. Knopf

Palazzo, T. (1954) *Aesop's Fables*. New York: Garden City Books

Parrinder, G. (1982) *Library of the world's myth's and legends: African mythology*. New York: Bedrick

Paley, V. G. (1997). *The girl with the brown crayon*. Harvard University Press.

Patterson, J. (1991) *Angels, prophets, rabbis and kings from the stories of the Jewish people*. New York: Bedrick

Philip, N. (Ed., 1996) *American fairy tales*. New York: Hyperion

Poe, E. A. (1845/2010) *Complete stories and poems*. New York: Doubleday

Polette, N. (1994). *Eight Cinderellas: China, Egypt, Korea, Germany, Native American, Africa, Russia, Great Britain*. Dayton OH: Pieces of Learning, www.piecesoflearning.com.

Potter, B. (1905/2006)) *The complete tales of Beatrix Potter*. New York: F. Warne & Co.

Pratt, D. & Kula, E. *Magic animals of Japan*. (1967) Berkeley, CA: Parnassus Press

Ransome, A. (1916) *Old Peter's Russian tales*. Great Britain. Thomas Nelson

Roessel, M. *Songs from the Navajo tradition: A Navajo girl learns to weave*. (1995) MN: Lerner

Rowling, J.K. (2009) *Harry Potter: The complete series*. New York: Thorndike Press

Sakado, F. & Hayashi, Y. (1959/2005) *Japanese children's favorite stories: Book two*. Boston, Vermont, Tokyo: Tuttle

San Souci, R. (1989) *The talking eggs*. New York: Dial

San Souci, R. (1992) *Sukey and the mermaid*. New York: Aladdin

San Souci, R. (1998) *Cendrillon: A Caribbean Cinderella*. New York: Simon & Schuster.

Seoul International Publishing House (1986) *Two brothers and their magic gourds: A Korean folk story for children*. Author.

Sherlock, P. (1966) *West Indian folktales*. Oxford University Press

Sierra, J. (2000) *The gift of the crocodile*. New York: Simon & Schuster

Sierra, J. (1992) *The Oryx multicultural folktale series: Cinderella*. Arizona/Canada: Oryx Press

Steptoe, J. (1987) *Mufaro's beautiful daughters*. New York: Lothrop, Lee & Shepard Books.

Stevens, A. (1999) *Ariadne's clue: A guide to the symbols of mankind*. Princeton University Press.

Stokstad, M. *Art: A brief history* (3rd edition). 2007) New Jersey: Pearson Prentice Hall

Thompson, V.L. (1988) *Hawaiian myths of earth, sea, and sky*. University of Hawaii Press

Von Franz, M. L. (1975) *An introduction to the psychology of fairy tales*. New York, NY: Spring

Weinrich, B. S. (Ed. 1988)) *Yiddish folktales*. New York: Schocken Books

White, E. B. (1945) *Stuart Little*. New York: Harper Collins

Wilson, B. K. (1966) *Greek fairy tales*. Chicago: Follett

Yen Mah, A. (2005) *Chinese Cinderella and the secret dragon society*. New York: HarperCollins

Zipes, J. (2000) *The Oxford companion to fairy tales*. Oxford University Press

Zipes, J. (trans. 2003) *All new third edition*: *The complete fairy tales of the Brothers Grimm*. New York: Bantam Books

www.ingramcontent.com/pod-product-compliance
Lightning Source LLC
Chambersburg PA
CBHW030016290326
41934CB00005B/357